NOTHING
TO
PROVE

WHY WE CAN STOP
TRYING SO HARD

JENNIE
ALLEN

FOUNDER OF IF:GATHERING

WATERBR

NOTHING TO PROVE

All Scripture quotations, unless otherwise indicated, are taken from the ESV® Bible (the Holy Bible, English Standard Version®), copyright © 2001 by Crossway, a publishing ministry of Good News Publishers. Used by permission. All rights reserved. Scripture quotations marked (MSG) are taken from The Message. Copyright © by Eugene H. Peterson 1993, 1994, 1995, 1996, 2000, 2001, 2002. Used by permission of Tyndale House Publishers Inc. Scripture quotations marked (NIV) are taken from the Holy Bible, New International Version®, NIV®. Copyright © 1973, 1978, 1984 by Biblica Inc.® Used by permission. All rights reserved worldwide. Scripture quotations marked (NLT) are taken from the Holy Bible, New Living Translation, copyright © 1996, 2004, 2007, 2013, 2015 by Tyndale House Foundation. Used by permission of Tyndale House Publishers Inc., Carol Stream, Illinois 60188. All rights reserved.

Trade Paperback ISBN 978-1-60142-962-9
Hardcover ISBN 978-0-7352-9088-4
eBook ISBN 978-1-60142-963-6

Copyright © 2017 by Jennie Allen

Cover design by Kelly L. Howard and Lauren Sterrett; cover art by Anna Petyarre

Published in association with Yates & Yates, www.yates2.com.

Published in the United States by WaterBrook, an imprint of the Crown Publishing Group, a division of Penguin Random House LLC, New York.

WATERBROOK® and its deer colophon are registered trademarks of Penguin Random House LLC.

The Library of Congress has cataloged the original hardcover edition as follows:
Names: Allen, Jennie, author.
Title: Nothing to prove : why we can stop trying so hard / Jennie Allen.
Description: First edition. | Colorado Springs, Colorado : WaterBrook, 2017 | Includes biblio-
    graphical references.
Identifiers: LCCN 2016038222 (print) | LCCN 2016046536 (ebook) | ISBN 9781601429612
    (hardcover) | ISBN 9781601429636 (electronic)
Subjects: LCSH: Christian women—Religious life. | Self-confidence—Religious aspects—
    Christianity. | Self-perception—Religious aspects—Christianity. | Self-perception in women.
Classification: LCC BV4527 .A45 2017 (print) | LCC BV4527 (ebook) | DDC 248.8/43—dc23
LC record available at https://lccn.loc.gov/2016038222

Printed in the United States of America

10 9

SPECIAL SALES
Most WaterBrook books are available at special quantity discounts when purchased in bulk by corporations, organizations, and special-interest groups. Custom imprinting or excerpting can also be done to fit special needs. For information, please e-mail specialmarketscms@penguin randomhouse.com or call 1-800-603-7051.

Because of my two sisters (and best friends),
Brooke and Katie.

....

You two show me unconditional,
never-going-anywhere,
no-matter-what,
never-have-to-prove-a-thing
love.

Through thick and thin
we've tested that this year,
and God through you was solid.
Forever grateful for you.

Contents

Contents

Admitting Our Thirst

Jennie, why are you holding back?"

My closest friends always ask intrusive questions. Wedged into the backseat on our road trip to Houston right before Christmas, I gave my sound-bite answers, not wanting to take up too much of the oxygen in the car and knowing that my life, in comparison to so many, is just not as hard as it sometimes feels.

They didn't buy it. Bekah pressed in again. "I see it, Jennie. I see it on you and in you. You feel so much pressure. Where is the pressure coming from?"

I looked out the car window. Tears burned in my eyes, but I wouldn't let them fall. I couldn't decide if I actually wanted to go there and feel it all. As much as I tried to mean it when I declared, "I'm good," a steady, silent grief had been growing in recent months. It seemed my chest was always tight, and many nights I lay awake half afraid and half trying to trust God with things like . . .

. . . the nagging insecurities I carry, wondering if any of the ways I am spending my life even matter.

. . . the growing challenges we were facing with one of our kids and his special needs.

. . . the grief I feel for my baby sister, who is suffering through unthinkable tragedy.

. . . the inescapable pressures I feel as I lead a growing organization that has taken on a life of its own.

. . . the weariness that all of these pressures and more bring.

. . . the sin that is coming out of me toward people I love because of the stress of all of it.

Ugh. Do I go there? What good will it accomplish?

Wanting to keep my composure, I held back as we drove the few hours to Houston. I wanted to hide behind the familiar posturing that would shift everyone's attention onto the next topic.

I was silent, deciding.

But they weren't going to stop.

Subject change. "Let's stop and eat. Aren't you all hungry?"

They agreed to let me eat if I would open up and tell them how I was really doing. Held hostage by these crazy-good friends, I would have to risk being vulnerable.

Somehow in the posh suburbs of Houston, we found this little shack of a burger joint with a dirt floor and no central heat. We were the only ones there. We huddled around the outdoor heater and ate some of the best burgers we'd ever tasted.

To the constant concern of our darling waiter, who continually brought me napkins, I fell apart and with a lot of tears gave my friends access to all of me: the constant inadequacy I feel, the fears of letting down those I lead or, even worse, my kids, the constant pressure I try to ignore but never seem to escape, the grief for my sister, the doubt that I often feel toward God even though I preach and write books about Him, the way I had snapped earlier on a poor intern at the office, the constant feeling that no matter how hard I try, I cannot be enough. All the things I didn't want to say, didn't even want to admit to myself, I said them.

For two solid hours my friends gifted me all the oxygen. They sacrificially and without judgment handed it over and forced me to breathe it in, to lovingly receive it without fear. For the first time in a long time, I laughed hard and free. The deep, happy, make-fun-of-your-life-and-yourself kind of laughter.

For those two hours I let myself be a complete fool who didn't have an iota of her junk together. I was free of the expectations, the roles I play, the pressures of real life. Nothing about my circumstances changed in that moment. But everything on the inside shifted. I didn't realize until then that, accidentally, I'd let my life subtly turn into a performance. On that dirt floor, I forgot all of my lines, abandoned all of my roles, dropped all of the costumes . . .

I had nothing to prove.

I drank in grace. I hadn't known that was what I'd been so thirsty for. *Grace.* I didn't know until I confessed my thirst on a dirt floor over burgers. My friends had that grace stored up from the contagious grace of Jesus that they all know well. Like a cold stream, Jesus's grace poured out of them into my dry, weary, thirsty soul.

Maybe you've known that thirst, that deep-within-your-bones craving for relief? Maybe you feel it right now? I'm convinced every one of us is fighting some pressure, some suffering, some sin, some burden—perhaps all of those at the same time. Yet what do we all say when we're asked the question, "How are you?"

We say, "Okay. Fine. Great."

I have a secret for you: Nobody is *okay, fine, great.*

But, goodness, we are all tired of trying to pretend we are.

Are you tired? You are not alone.

The truth I found that day on the dirt floor outside Houston is available and true every day for every one of us. **We need a new way to live.**

Do you want off the stage? Guess what? A cheeseburger and a dirt-floor shack full of grace are waiting for you.

But I should warn you, there is a full-on war to keep you from finding it. If heaven and God and angels and demons are all real, then a real enemy is out to claim all that is good and free and peaceful and joyful in us.

So we start here. We start by realizing we are not alone. We start by recognizing that, indeed, all hell will be out to get us if we decide to live free and enjoy grace.

Ben Rector, one of my favorite musicians, often puts words to music in a way that expresses truth. He wrote, "Sometimes the devil sounds a lot like Jesus."[1]

We've been deceived by the lies of an enemy who knows exactly how to twist our thirst to his purposes. And we desperately need to open our eyes to his perverse tactics.

IF I WERE YOUR ENEMY . . .

If I were your enemy, this is what I would do:

Make you believe you need permission to lead.

Make you believe you are helpless.

Make you believe you are insignificant.

Make you believe that God wants your decorum and behavior.

And for years these lies have been sufficient to shut down much of the church.

But now many of you are awake. You are in the Word and on your knees. God is moving through you, and you are getting dangerous. You are starting to get free and leading other people to freedom. The old lies are no longer adequate.

So if I were your enemy, I would make you numb and distract you from God's story.

Technology, social media, Netflix, travel, food and wine, comfort. I would not tempt you with notably bad things, or you would get suspicious. I would distract you with everyday comforts that slowly feed you a different story and make you forget God.

Then you would dismiss the Spirit leading you, loving you, and comforting you. Then you would start to love comfort more than surrender and obedience and souls.

If that didn't work, **I would attack your identity. I would make you believe you had to prove yourself.**

Then you would focus on yourself instead of God.

Friends would become enemies.

Teammates would become competition.

You would isolate yourself and think you are not enough.

You would get depressed and be ungrateful for your story.

Or,

You would compare and believe you are better than others.

You would judge people who need God.

You would condemn them rather than love and invite them in.

You would gossip and destroy and tear down other works of God.

Either way you would lose your joy, because your eyes would be fixed on yourself and people instead of on Jesus.

And if that didn't work, **I would intoxicate you with the mission of God rather than God Himself.**

Then you would worship a cause instead of Jesus.

You would fight each other to have the most important roles.

You would burn out from striving.

You would think that success is measured by the results you see.

You would build platforms for applause rather than to display God.

Then all your time and effort would be spent on becoming important rather than on knowing Jesus and loving people. The goals would be to gather followers, earn fancy job titles, publish books, build big ministries rather than to seek the souls of men and the glory of God.

And if that didn't work, **I would make you suffer.**

Then maybe you would think God is evil rather than good.

Your faith would shrink.

You would get bitter and weary and tired rather than flourish and grow and become more like Christ.

You would try to control your life rather than step into the plans He has for you.

The enemy is telling you that freedom is only found in finally proving to yourself and to the world that . . .

you are important.

you are in control.

you are liked.

you are happy.

you are enough.

EXPOSING THE LIE

Here is the thing. The enemy promises water, but every time we go to his wells, they are empty. He gives us a sip of water, enough that we keep believing him. We have believed the lie that our cravings will be satisfied if we are enough and if we have enough. So we chase image, answers, things, people—and we wonder all the while, *Why am I still thirsty?*

God is clear in the book of Jeremiah about what is happening:

My people have committed two sins:
They have forsaken me,
    the spring of living water,
and have dug their own cisterns,
    broken cisterns that cannot hold water.[2]

Water. No human can survive three days without it. No other resource is more essential to sustain life. None.

When you look at maps of some of the most arid places in the world, you find the cities all along rivers and streams of water. **Where**

there is water, there is life. Vegetation, animals, industry, human flourishing. **And in the absence of water, there is death.**

I don't think you would have picked up this book if you didn't feel thirsty. I believe you are here because you are so thirsty you can't stand it anymore and you pray that maybe this time you will find living, lasting water for life. I am here because I want to fight for you to live, no longer thirsty but filled. I found water. I found rest. And I will show you where it lives.

There is water for you. Not just enough to quench your thirst but an unlimited supply that will fill you and then come pouring out of you into a thirsty world. But the water you need is found in only one Source.

I'll tell you right up front, there is no secret here. Just one answer to your thirst:

Jesus.

"If anyone is thirsty, let him come to me and drink," He says in the gospel of John. "Whoever believes in me . . . streams of living water will flow from within him."[3]

He alone is the Source from which flows all the things we crave and hope to become.

I love that I can begin here, making no empty promises. Because my single goal is to lead your thirsty soul to streams of living water, to Jesus. He always delivers.

Why go here?

Practically speaking, nothing I am facing in my life changed that day on the dirt floor in Houston. And yet everything changed.

I didn't feel so alone.

I felt relief.

I felt loved.

I felt like I could take a deep breath.

I felt known.

I believed Jesus more. That He forgives and is in this all with me.

I felt the groundswell of freedom that comes from living with Nothing. To. Prove.

I should warn you that finding our way out of the desert of striving and pressure will not be easy. But I hope you'll come with me anyway. I'll show you how I found my way out.

Let's start at the beginning, when I learned to chase mirages of water in the desert . . .

Part 1

·····················

OUR DESERT
OF STRIVING

My Quiet Confession

The voice has been in my head most of my life.

I am not enough.

He hoisted me up on his lap, and my twelve-year-old scrawny legs dangled over the arm of his worn plaid recliner. Daddy is a dreamer, and this is where we dreamed. His six-foot frame easily collapsed the chair into position, and the two of us stared at the popcorn ceiling and analyzed the world together.

"Any boys paying attention to you, Jennie?"

I offered an obligatory giggle because that was a silly thought at twelve. Soon after, boys *would* become the object of my most obsessive interest, but not yet. Not only was I lanky, but my grandmother had cut my hair down to the nub only a year before. I'm sure her intention wasn't as unkind as it felt. Then she cocked her head and decided it would look even better with a perm.

My elegant silver-haired grandmother and my fifth-grade self had matching hairdos.

So no, Dad. There were no boys. Well, except for Henry, whose blond mop of hair was wilder than his behavior. After my tragic fifth-grade hair incident, Henry kindly asked if my hair had been sucked off by a vacuum cleaner.

Yep. That still stings a bit.

Daddy and I dreamed and wondered. Grades. Friends. Sports. Boys. He rattled off subjects as if they were part of a secret directory of things daddies everywhere are given to ask their daughters when it becomes difficult to converse with them.

The list wasn't meant to catalog all his expectations; he was just checking in, helping his awkward little darting-eyed girl set goals and find her place. Mostly he was prying, though I only know it now that I've parented a few twelve-year-olds of my own. He couldn't know that at the time, my little first-born brain was racing to assimilate the list and, with it, taking note of a line just beyond my reach. A thick black finish line that marked the place I would accomplish this growing list of imagined and unachievable expectations.

That line would wait indefinitely in the distant border of my mind, enticing me to reach it. Within me, for most of my life, would live a theory that I assumed was a fact: It was possible to arrive at a destination where I would finally prove myself. I would *arrive* at the line marking the place where I finally measured up to my family, my peers, my God, and my own expectations. But like the mirage in the desert, every time I thought I finally was closing in, the line backed itself up.

It all started before I was old enough to notice or be noticed by the boys, when the thought first occurred to me . . .

I was not enough.

During my freshman year at the University of Arkansas, some friends coerced me into joining them in a long line for the Razorbacks cheerleader tryouts. Obviously I was not going to make it—I wasn't much of an athlete. There was the one season of soccer in first grade. Then I tried to run track one year and melodramatically yet genuinely fainted after running the 800 m in my first meet. I did take gymnastics, but I never made the cheerleading squad until my senior year of high school. I don't know if I wasn't good enough or if I made myself so nauseously nervous that I didn't smile. In any case, I knew I wouldn't make it on the college level, but it felt fun to pretend for a few days that I could.

Growing up in Arkansas, I'd gone with my dad to all the Razorbacks games, and what did I do? I didn't watch the boys in pads on the field. Along with a lot of the other little girls in the stadium, I memorized every move the cheerleaders made. Now here I was standing in that line with some of the most darling, athletic girls I'd ever seen, all wearing their National Cheerleaders Association instructor shirts. They held résumés listing every award they'd won and each special team they'd graced.

I had no résumé. One year as a high school cheerleader didn't justify a résumé.

I almost walked away, but I stayed. Despite my lack of résumé, I somehow accidentally made cheerleader in college. Now, I realize you may be put off by these seemingly random stories from my early life with blond boys named Henry and cheerleading tryouts, but hang with me. The world doesn't wait until you reach a certain age to issue you an identity. From childhood we begin defining ourselves by the loudest messages.

Anyway, with a red little hog on my face and a tiny uniform and inadequacy and fear as near and dear companions, I arrived at my first practice along with the girls who deserved to be there. I felt like a fraud. Add to it that, despite my unremarkable height of five foot three, somehow in the world of college cheerleaders I was one of the tallest.

It all just felt like a tremendous mistake.

Our coach led us up to the second floor of the gym we would soon call home for three to four hours each day. The second floor stretched out down a long white hallway with doors leading to offices. The only thing visible at the end of the hallway was a medical scale. We lined up and stepped on the rickety metal scale. The coach held a clipboard and scribbled down our weight beside each of our names. She would go on to do this every six weeks for the next several years of my life. If our weight crept up from that point more than a few pounds, the coaches would tell us to lose weight or be benched. That only happened to me once.

Then a little girl who never felt lovely enough met a college career of scales and began a deep tailspin into a five-year eating disorder and obsession to try to control her appearance.

All because of the dark familiar line in the distance reminding me . . .

I was not enough.

———

"People don't think about you as much as you think they do." My practical mom used to reassure me of this when I was in seventh grade and built massive conspiracy theories about why I didn't get invited to crucial social events such as Stephanie Angelo's end-of-year sleepover. She meant it to be comforting. And strangely it was. I never wanted to be the object of people's thoughts; it seemed too risky when my oxygen was their approval.

Then I became a pastor's wife. And guess what? My mom's middle school mantra failed me. Because people definitely thought about me more than I wished they did. Whether our kids attended public or private school. How we spent our money. How our kids behaved. Who our friends were. How my husband was leading and even what attire he wore. All these topics and more were regularly brought to my attention or questioned.

Most weekends my husband, Zac, was busy prepping sermons, and every Sunday morning he was gone before I was even awake. Usually Conner, my oldest, was up first and the other two kids would follow. Each week brought renewed fights over brushing hair and teeth and what everyone should wear. Eventually I gave up on idealistic concepts such as hair bows. My earnest dream was to arrive at church on time, but it was rarely realized.

Eventually kids were wrangled into their Sunday school classes, and I began the walk down the hall to the meet-and-greet called church.

I've never been great at meet-and-greets, but as a pastor's wife, I came to fear them.

You may find it helpful to know that I have a condition called attention deficit disorder (ADD). I know a lot of people joke about having ADD, but for those of us who actually have it, our brains work differently than everyone else's. My ADD makes it difficult to focus in rooms full of people. I guess most people's brains can ignore the other conversations happening, the baby crying, the worship that has already started in the gym, the footsteps coming up behind you. But I can't. I hear everything.

ADD brains have two modes: one is called hyperfocus, the ability to zero in on one thing so completely that it is as if not one other thing exists on the whole earth, as if I am in a completely other world. The other mode is that the brain moves so quickly from one thing to the next that it is nearly impossible to focus on anything. If I am in control of a situation, for instance you and I are having a quiet conversation over coffee, I can turn on my hyperfocus drive and you would never know I have ADD. But a meet-and-greet is torture for my brain. A simple conversation becomes a daunting challenge, especially after managing three young kids all morning.

Each Sunday after dropping off the kids, I walked down the hall of our church plant full of dread. The people were not the problem; I adored the people. Their seeming expectations of me were the problem. I desperately wanted to prove to them that I was an asset to Zac in the way I cared for our people. When you plant a church, there are no buildings, no programs, no history to help visitors assess whether this church is a good fit, so people often decide if they want to stay based on the pastor and his vision and his wife.

Do we trust the pastor and his wife? Do we like them? Can I follow them? I knew that each week in our small growing church, most people were asking themselves these questions.

Todd must have passed me in that hallway when I was full of dread. He likely said hi to me and smiled. I didn't smile back—because I didn't hear him say hi.

One week I got a call from Todd's wife. "Are you upset with us?"

Nothing could be further from the truth. They were some of our easiest friends. Why was Rachel asking me this?

Rachel went on, "Todd says he has tried to speak to you several times on Sunday mornings in the hallway, and you always ignore him."

Trust me, passive-aggressive is just not my shtick. If anything, I am probably *too* direct when something is bothering me. Of course I wasn't mad and ignoring Todd, but how could I explain all the pressure I felt on Sundays to measure up and perform? How could I describe what it felt like to walk into church with three barely dressed kids and a church full of people deciding if we were enough for them? How could I tell her I have ADD and I didn't even hear Todd multiple weeks in a row?

So I didn't. I just apologized and assured her we were great.

But from that point on when I walked down that hallway, I added to my growing list of pressure-soaked to-dos: smile and say hi to every person I pass.

I was not enough.

My kids' school sent an e-mail asking to meet. Across from me, three administrators sat with their prepared notes, and I sat helpless and completely ill prepared.

"Your child is not succeeding, and we wonder if he is getting the help he needs at home?"

"We know you work and travel a lot."

"We know you all are so busy."

While the words were said kindly, they expressed my worst fears: *I am not enough.*

I am not doing enough.

I am not measuring up as a mother.

My child is not measuring up, and it is my fault.

I ached to offer my genuine explanations: *I could not love this kid any more than I do. I am always helping him with schoolwork. Oh, how I pray for him. I have missed so much work trying to get him the right help.*

I didn't say anything.

Instead, I fought back tears and stifled all my inadequate defenses. I listened. I asked questions. And then I walked out and collapsed in tears in the driver's seat of my car. I couldn't breathe. I drove home and ran past Zac, who looked at me to ask who was taking Kate, our fourteen-year-old, to track practice. I couldn't answer. I was just looking for somewhere to hide.

I lay down on the floor of my closet, grabbed a dirty T-shirt from the floor, and hid my face in it. I cried harder than any human should. When I finally took a deep breath and dried the tears and opened my eyes, my first thought was, *Dang, my closet is a wreck!*

My breath was gone and the tears in the T-shirt were back. Leave it to a disaster of a closet to push me over the edge.

I was not enough.

For so many years the voice has been in my head: *I am not enough.*

Is it possible you hear that same voice?

Maybe you've never struggled with an eating disorder or with the pressures of being a pastor's wife, but I'm convinced nearly all of us feel this incredible pressure to prove we measure up in some way. Every morning we face the list of tasks left undone the previous night, the expectations of our family and coworkers, the burden to be the beautiful, strong, and gracious ideal humans that we're convinced the world, the church, and God require. We sense that somewhere, with everyone watching, is an ominous scale and a clipboard recording our results. We all fight feelings of inadequacy.

We walk around desperately afraid we don't measure up. We slap on self-esteem strategies that feel a little like playing pretend dress up when we were seven. We think that we are someone grown up and lovely and accomplished, and we want to be someone grown up and lovely and accomplished.

But deep in our marrow, we know it is pretend. We are not enough.

So we spend our lives trying to shift that reality.

God has a different story line for us, one in which our souls are content and epic stories unfold through our lives here—but not because of us.

In spite of us.

Romans is pretty clear about our reality: "For all have sinned and fall short of the glory of God."[1]

But what if we have everything backward? What if there was a story where the ones who aren't enough, the ones who recognize they don't measure up, are the very ones the God of the universe picks to move wildly in and through?

What if I told you today you could stop trying so hard and simply rest?

What if I told you today you could start enjoying yourself and your life without performing or striving for another minute?

What if I told you that you don't measure up? And that it's okay. In fact, it's necessary.

———

I didn't go out looking for a big vision for my life. I woke up the night of my thirtieth birthday and couldn't sleep. I couldn't shake the phrase spinning through my mind: *disciple a generation.* It was a silly thought. I was a mom of young kids and a pastor's wife of a small church. I didn't have a platform or influence. I didn't even have a Twitter account. What was I supposed to do with this?

I remember for two days it felt as if my bones hurt, I was so burdened by what God wanted me to do with such a ridiculously nebulous and enormous task. I mentioned it to a few good friends, who wisely told me, "If this is God, Jennie, He will make it happen."

I agreed there was no clear step to take, so I laid that burden aside and moved on with my already full life.

Then a few years later my husband and I began praying a simple prayer: "Anything, God." Convicted by the life of Katie Davis—she was living in Uganda and had adopted multiple girls off the streets, laying down her life in such a way it was contagious—we surrendered every part of our lives to Jesus in a more terrifying absolute way than we ever had before. "Anything, God." We prayed it, and God initiated the kind of events my friends had said to wait on. God started to open doors I wasn't even knocking on.

I'd been teaching a Bible study in my home for years. But I knew I held back and kept it small, always inviting only a few safe friends. But, goodness, I loved teaching the Bible. I always have. The moment I came home from summer camp after trusting Christ, I seemingly instinctively gathered a handful of younger girls and started teaching them the book of Revelation. Hysterical. I know now that probably wasn't the best choice. But teaching the Bible was and is like breathing for me.

Yet navigating the pressures of being a pastor's wife seemed enough, and choosing more leadership seemed terrifying because leading always coexists tightly with criticism. My skin was so desperately thin. But I knew I wanted to please God and quit living for other people's opinions. So in the fall of 2009 for the first time I took the risk of opening the doors of our study to any women who wanted to attend while I taught *Stuck,* a study I had written for some women in my living room. They came—150 people from different backgrounds and age groups came together. People trusted Christ for the first time. Women were freed of bondage they'd fought for decades, and they were starting to have their own convictions and dreams to serve God. Obedience seemed to be contagious. God was moving in our little corner of the world in a way I had not seen since college.

And only one year later, without much effort on my part, I was given opportunities to publish my studies and speak on some of the biggest stages in Christendom. The girl terrified of 150 people's opinions now would have to face one hundred thousand of them. These were never the goals or the dreams I had.

God was shoving me out of every comfort I craved. I didn't want to deal with opinions and judgment, I didn't want to risk appearing arrogant, I didn't want to make Zac uncomfortable, and I didn't want to miss the familiar easy rhythms I enjoyed with my kids.

Yet the words *disciple a generation* continued to echo in me. I couldn't shake the sense that God was causing these opportunities to unfold for purposes beyond my understanding and certainly beyond my fears.

I began having small, seemingly insignificant conversations in which I shared some of the dreams and hopes I felt stirring. The question I couldn't shake was this: IF God is real, then how are we going to live like it? And thousands of women around the world responded, drawn to the beauty of what it would mean to dream together about how to unleash our faith. IF:Gathering was born.

Our first gathering launched to an immediate sellout, and then women around the world rose up and rallied to lead gatherings in their homes and churches and cities. Within a short while, an army of women was coming together around the name of Jesus to use their gifts and spend their lives discipling the world. We were working hard and doing our best to pursue God with excellence, but it often seemed we were making more wrong decisions than right ones. Yet despite the chaos of our inexperience and missteps, the vision was resonating. IF was beginning to take on a life of its own, and I was mostly just terrified. I was desperately afraid I was not equipped to lead this.

The world saw a powerful, gorgeous work of God uniting women to obey and follow Jesus, but behind the scenes, IF also was costing us many of the things I most feared: relational conflict and personal rejection and disappointment and an overwhelming amount of time and energy required to lead this growing vision.

I wanted nothing more than to please God. Yet the intensity of the growing army was pushing me into more and more places I felt ill equipped to lead, and I wasn't sure how much longer I could pretend to be holding this together. I desperately feared that the words always bouncing around my head were true:

I am not a leader. I am not cut out for this. I. CAN. NOT. DO. THIS. God, You picked the wrong girl.

I am just not enough.

And the more IF kept growing, the more I feared that a whole lot of people would find that out.

Nine years after the sleepless night that brought the weighty conviction to *disciple a generation,* IF was no longer just a dream. I found myself behind a curtain peering out at women who'd come hungry and expectant, wanting more of God. It was our third time to gather, and now over one million women in more than one hundred countries watched and waited for the video broadcast to begin.

Six steps were all that separated me from the stage.

It did not help that this was one of the biggest stages in music history. Wrapping the backstage halls of Austin City Limits at the Moody Theater were iconic images of some of the greatest artists of all time, all who have commanded this same stage. Willie Nelson. Mumford and Sons. Diana Ross. They haunted me. They mocked me. This is *the* music stage of Texas. This is the stage the greats play.

They all must have walked up these steps with confidence equivalent to their brilliant talent and gifts.

I kept staring at the steps and wondering what would happen at the top, when I looked past the heavy black curtains and into the waiting eyes. The world would say to me, "You are successful. You've done it. You are finally enough." Yet I will tell you a secret. As I stood on what should have been miles past the thick black line of my expectations, it still loomed just out of reach, mocking me. *Enough* is a mirage that cannot be caught. You and I can keep chasing it, or we can quit the childish game the enemy taught us young.

In that moment I could have owned what the world was telling me. It would have been nice to agree for just a moment that maybe I had arrived, that I am a confident leader with a crystal-clear vision. But standing there, I knew that I was not . . .

brave enough . . .

smart enough . . .

gifted enough . . .

sure enough . . .

strong enough . . .

to lead this movement.

I knew I was not enough.

Six steps. I walked up them, and that day, rather than pretend I was enough, I stood on that historic stage and I let out my quiet confession in front of more than a million people.

I am not enough. And I am done trying to be.

It was one of the most peaceful and freeing moments of my life.

While God may not be prompting you to announce your inadequacy from a stage, I'm going to guess that something in your life requires more than you can deliver.

Maybe you are in a difficult marriage and every day is a struggle. Maybe you are buried in debt and unpaid bills. Maybe you have a child with special needs that requires you to wade deep into complicated paperwork, psychologists and psychiatrists, and therapies. Maybe one of your parents is slowly fading into dementia. Maybe you feel paralyzed with anxiety or isolated by depression.

Whatever it is that set your world reeling, how will you move forward? Striving, pretending, white knuckling—or free? My dream is that you would embrace your worst fears head on and find that our God is enough for them. My prayer is for you to start enjoying the freedom that comes when we quit trying to prove ourselves, when we surrender what is out of control to the One who is in control.

We strive to be seen, to be known, to matter. We're desperate to believe we are doing a good job at whatever has been entrusted to us.

But we are not enough. We are not God. We don't have all the answers, all the wisdom, all the strength, all the energy. We are finite, sinful beings. And that is okay.

In fact, it is the confession that unleashes the freedom we are aching for.

Star Charts and Backpacks

Our son Cooper was nearly four years old the day we met him for the first time. I think in my head I was flying to Africa to bring home my cuddly toddler, only to arrive and realize this toddler was a full-blown kid who had learned how to rule his roost at the orphanage. We'd had no input on any of the 1,400 days of his life so far, then—*bam!*—just like that, he was our son.

When we brought Coop back to our darling little cinder-block guest home in Rwanda, words poured out of him without any apparent concern that none of his new family in the room had any idea what he was saying. That first night I cooked "popeyes" for dinner on a tiny skillet. I grew up in Arkansas eating popeyes: over-medium eggs, with the yellow yolk poking out of a little hole in toast. Cooking them that night in Rwanda for our new person felt anything but familiar and nostalgic.

The typical thick porridge he ate in the orphanage didn't require utensils, but popeyes pretty much do. When I reached to show him how the fork worked, he knocked it away. Zac quickly corrected him with words Coop couldn't yet understand but in a tone that he apparently did. That child stood up and started waving his finger and preaching like he was in an Alabama church. Our strong-willed, gregarious new son was obviously familiar with a good old-fashioned southern scolding.

If this was a showdown of wills, I was pretty sure who would win. In view of our conviction not to spank our son who was trying to attach to even the idea of parents, we needed a way to motivate his cooperation.

We soon landed back home in the States, where he entered a world that he could not have begun to imagine during his years in an African orphanage. High-top shoes, Fanta slushes at Sonic, *Pingu* on repeat on Netflix, swimming pools with inflatable rafts that looked like sharks. But he had one obsession: my three bigger kids all had bikes, and Cooper wanted one. So I got online, printed a picture of the most epic bike any four-year-old had ever seen, and I made rows of squares with an arrow pointing to the bike. Whenever Coop did anything noteworthy—used the potty, used a fork, stayed in bed, shared his toys—he earned a metallic little star sticker toward that bike.

And I will be honest: it worked.

In fact, that star chart still works. He can't do math to save his life until there is a light saber at the end of ten Teenage Mutant Ninja Turtles stickers. Then he can do long division in second grade. While this brings out the best in Coop's behavior and performance, in some ways it also brings out the worst.

My Coop fights shame. Somewhere along the way in that Rwandan orphanage, Coop decided he was a bad kid. So on the days he earns a star, a bright crooked grin breaks out, as if this star proved he was wrong about himself and maybe he is good. But if he doesn't land his star, his head drops, as if the finger-waving scoldings from the orphanage are all true. Yes, Coop wants enough stickers for his light saber, but this ache is bigger. Something in him strives to prove he is enough.

As a mama, I don't want my kid to feel defined by stars or empty boxes, and yet we live in a world that issues gold stars and, more often, the finger-waving scolding shame.

We all have our own version of star charts, something we are trying to get approval for, from our parents, friends, spouses, kids, online acquaintances, coworkers, or even from God. Most of us carry that striving feeling all our lives.

Unrealistic expectations we impose on ourselves are set in motion from nearly the moment we come into the world. We learn young that the harder we work and the better we perform, the more rewards and applause we get. In school, the harder we work, the more approval we get. Our parents are on the sidelines of our lives cheering, "You got an A!" or frowning, "You got a C? What happened?" At work, those with the best performance usually get promoted.

We learn to want to win at everything. It isn't bad or wrong; it's just the way the world works. The benefit of these "charts" is that we do learn the principle of reaping and sowing. We learn that when we study, we make good grades. When we are a good friend, people are a good friend back. When we are generous and forgiving with our siblings, they are more likely to be generous and forgiving with us. These cause-and-effect life lessons are good to learn.

But the way we interact with our parents and our teachers and our bosses eventually makes its way into our spiritual lives. So often we try to relate to God through star charts—and we end up feeling shame or disappointment that our performance didn't bring the outcome we wanted. We constantly try to work harder, to achieve more, to jump farther, to score higher in order to win His approval or His blessing. We end up relating to God with an underlying fear rather than full of expectant, childlike, joy-filled faith.

God does not work with star charts. He is not manipulated by our performance. My friend Sally, who is fighting breast cancer, did not in some way disappoint God and get cancer.

Sadly, because life is hard and most of us don't feel like we are knocking it out of the park for God or anyone else, we live a bit afraid that when God looks our way, He is disappointed.

TRAVELING HEAVY

I wish my own journey from striving to freedom was as simple as six steps and a public confession, but the freedom to confess on that stage in that moment was built on a thousand other moments with God, moments where He invited me to stop striving.

For example, adoption comes with piles of paperwork and books. The paperwork you push through; the books often scare off anyone who's feeling halfhearted about this way of growing a family.

They tell you about the potential challenges your child who has experienced trauma could face; there may be rages and food hoarding and sleep difficulties. And they emphasize how vital it is that as a new adoptive parent, you cope with all that just right.

We'd been home for several months and Coop's English skills were coming along. But I noticed I felt as if I were carrying a heavy backpack. A new pressure was growing in me. Cooper's needs were unlike the needs I'd grown familiar with in my other kids, so parenting the way I'd always done was actually hurting him, pushing him away.

One day I yelled. Yep. Lose-your-mind kind of screaming at our darling, confused, doing-his-best-to-adjust-to-a-whole-new-world little boy. Not good for attachment bonding.

I remember the trailer for the movie *Wild*, seeing Reese Witherspoon's character carrying a backpack as big or bigger than she is. That is exactly what my life felt like.

I deeply wanted to be enough for my son; I wanted and needed him to feel loved. Adding to that weight was the familiar struggle with fear of people and the fact that I had been to Africa. Seeing Africa—both the beauty and the need—wrecked me forever. I couldn't escape images of boys Cooper's age running beside me, no parents in sight, with bellies distended, begging us for *bonbons,* meaning "candy."

I was drowning in all the need right in front of me but haunted by needs around the globe.

I found myself caught up in fear of God. Fear I would let Him down, fear I wasn't doing enough for those He loves. At the end of my life and at the end of the day, I just wanted to be enough for Him.

I'd begun to think, *God is so real and there is so much need in the world and it all feels so important and like we might screw up His plans or miss His plans.* An urgency began to consume my life and add weight to my deep-seated "not-enoughness." Friends who had also adopted weighed in with their strong opinions about parenting methods. Others we love wondered if we were crazy for disrupting our lives like this and worried aloud that his needs may distract us from giving our other kids all they need. Their words fed a growing narrative in my mind: *I could mess this up. It all depends on me.*

My backpack was so heavy, all I could think about was when I could take it off. But because this pack contained some good things, God things, I didn't even know if it was all right to take it off. I had strapped onto my shoulders the mission of God in this world.

I wanted Him to be proud of me.

Do you ever feel this way? Do you know that this is not even a thought in God's mind? This is not how the heavenly Father works. Sometimes earthly fathers expect us to earn their approval. But God doesn't work this way.

In Jeremiah He says, "Let not the wise man boast in his wisdom, let not the mighty man boast in his might, let not the rich man boast in his riches, but let him who boasts boast in this, that he understands and knows me, that I am the Lord who practices steadfast love, justice, and righteousness in the earth. For in these things I delight, declares the Lord."[1]

God is not after great performances or great movements. He is after us!

God already knows we are not enough, but He's not asking us to be. We are the ones who have chosen to walk through the desert with enormous packs strapped to our backs full of everything *but* water. As if the kingdom of God were held up or together by us.

So I propose a great experiment. What if together we name the junk we are carrying around and figure out what to do with it? What if we name our limitations, our fears, our imperfections, our striving, our sins, rather than try to escape them? Now take some time with this. Really stop and reflect and ask yourself these questions. It may help to sit down with a friend and work through them.

What is heavy for you right now?

What are you afraid of?

Can you identify some things you may be carrying?

I am going to give you all kinds of lovely suggestions, because if you are anything like me, you rarely stop long enough to even know how you are, much less identify what is wrong.

Name what's in your backpack.

Maybe it is in one of the following categories.

Fear

I don't know what I have to offer.

I don't know what I should do.

I feel helpless.

I am too old.

I am too young.

I am going to miss important things.

I am going to fail.

I am going to look like a fool.

People will get mad.

I won't be liked.

I am not strong enough.

My biggest fear is _____.

Difficulties

My life feels out of control.

My child is rebelling.

I can't do this.

I don't want to be a burden.

I am divorced.

I am sick.

People I love are suffering.

I don't want to appear weak.

My most difficult circumstance is _____.

Pressures

I can't measure up.

I am too weak.

I feel worthless.

I feel like it is up to me.

If I don't do it, it won't get done.

I don't know how to get it all done.

I am too busy.

There is too much to do, so why try?

I feel unlovable.

I feel like people love me for what I do and not who I am.

I don't have enough faith.

What if I fail?

My biggest pressure is _____.

Shame

I have messed up.

I'm not worthy.

I hope no one ever discovers the truth.

I can't believe I let that happen.

If people knew what I have done, they would reject me.

I am disqualified.

I have to hide.

I can't lead or move forward from this.

I am a fraud.

My biggest mistake that haunts me is _____.

We begin by naming because we trust that God is enough for whatever we are about to say. God is not surprised by our failures and disappointments and baggage. They are actually reminders of our need for God. He will use whatever means possible just to get to you and to be with you.

Name where you are not enough, where you are inadequate, and the junk you are carrying. Right now. Name it. Confess it. Call a good friend and talk about it. You have to admit you are wearing a backpack before you can find the freedom to take it off.

I began to have victory over my addiction to people's approval when I finally started calling my people pleasing *sin*. When I realized I had been worshipping people instead of God, that broke me. As I saw it for the idolatry it was, I lost my appetite for it.

Perhaps you, too, are carrying a burden that is flat-out sin. And sin requires repentance, not just confession. Repentance is a turning away from. Flee from it. Even if the burden is hidden in your thought life, Scripture calls us to "take captive every thought to make it obedient to Christ."[2] We fight sin. And we receive grace and we believe grace is enough to eradicate it.

But maybe your burden involves suffering in some way that is not in your control. Let me begin by saying I am so sorry. You may be facing illness or a spouse cheating on you or worse. It may feel like you can't take it off or lay it down. It is just with you and there may be no sign of it working out on this earth.

I have walked through unthinkable suffering with my best friend and my sister in the past three years. *I hate suffering!* But I have seen God be good in the midst of it. Jesus is better than happy stories that work out perfectly. He has been enough for the people closest to me, so much so that I can say confidently, He is enough for you too.

The enemy often pushes us out so far in the desert, we wonder if we will ever know joy again. But God promises, "I will lead you beside still waters. I will restore your soul."[3]

So Now What?

Now before you go and feel guilty for whatever your backpack contains, just stop. It's bad enough that we lug around these packs without adding our guilt for doing so.

God forgives our sin immediately and once and for all. He does not hold resentments or keep a tally of our wrongs. Psalm 103:12 says that the love of God is so great and vast that He has "removed our sins as far from us as the east is from the west."[4] This is such a hard concept for us to embrace because we are grudge holders. We label and define people based on their sin. If someone cheats, then he is a cheater. If she lies, then she is a liar.

But with God, when a sin has been confessed, it is forgiven once and for all. There is no labeling; there is not even a reminder of our past mistakes. There are no reparations for us to make because nothing in us earns His grace. It is offered free. EVERY. SINGLE. TIME. Any thought that tells us to lug our backpacks of shame and guilt is a direct attempt from the enemy to plant the suspicion that we aren't really forgiven.

Your eyes may still feel glued to the carpet with fear and shame, but God has a sneaky way of not only forgiving our past sin but redeeming the choices we thought had ruined everything. Goodness, I like Him.

One night recently in Austin, at the close of our Bible study, a woman I'll call Joanna came and found me. She walked up to me with her eyes glued to the carpet. Her dark messy hair was haphazardly pulled back out of her face. She was wearing an old, faded T-shirt that was two sizes too big. Something about her—actually almost everything about her—looked defeated.

In an effort to get to her eyes and to whatever heavy thing this woman was shouldering, I squatted down on the stairs at the front of the church. She followed my lead and sat down, but continued to look at the floor. She said, "I wanted you to know I just told my small group something that I have never told anybody in my whole life that happened to me when I was fourteen."

My heart quickly divided in half. One half broke because my guess is that Joanna is in her early forties. That means whatever just came out, she has been carrying for nearly three decades of her life. The other half of my heart flooded with hope that this could be the moment her life shifts. It could be the start of freedom.

My eyes stung with tears as she shared how terrified she felt at the thought that near strangers now know her deepest secret, a secret her husband doesn't even know. I couldn't land on what was ahead for her, so the only next right move seemed to be to grab her hands and talk to God. After amens, I encouraged her to find a counselor and to consider telling her husband about this heavy thing she had been carrying alone. I still don't know what Joanna shared that night. Maybe it was abuse, maybe it was an abortion . . . I don't know and I didn't need to know. But someone did.

Three weeks later, Joanna ran up to me and looked directly in my eyes. She told me about counseling. She told me about her husband, about his grace and how he wept when she shared this burden with him. She said, "Jennie, my husband and I have never been closer. I have never been more free."

Her entire physical appearance had changed in three weeks. Everything about her looked free.

But she had to name what she was carrying before she could ever get free of it. And you and I have to do the same if we want to ditch our backpacks.

I want to be clear: This will take courage. Because **to get to the place where God can be enough, we have to first admit we aren't.** Pretending we are okay—that is how a lot of us are making life work. With that illusion gone, we might have to live needing God.

And it might be hard.

Strike that. It is hard.

No more performing. No more pretending. No more proving ourselves.

It sounds good—until we have to say out loud the things we barely even want to come to mind.

We struggle in the dark with our backpacks filled with weights that we never name. And we're doing it alone. And we're doing it disconnected rather than looking into each other's eyes and saying, "I'm dying here." If we could just utter the words, somebody could speak the truth of grace over us. They could remind us of God and His love for us and pray for us and, for goodness' sake, fight for us.

Instead, we are letting the enemy take us down.

So my prayer is that you and I would believe rightly about God and about ourselves. Then can you imagine what will happen?

I can tell you what will happen: you'll start to be free and you'll start to love God again and you'll start to love your life again, no matter what it brings. It isn't easy, but it sure is a lot less hard. Maybe the reason you aren't free is that you are trying so hard?

What if we tore up our star charts and threw them away?

What if we quit performing?

What if we learned to let go of what we cannot control?

What if we started enjoying our life and our God again?

What if we stopped doing things for God and started doing them with God?

When we make that shift, we will be different. Because when we are with Him, we see Him for who He is and He changes us.

This is a journey into greater faith. Believing God and who He says

He is and who He says we are. It is a journey into a life of not trying so hard. It is a road to enjoying our abundant God rather than working so hard for Him.

When God freed the Israelites from Egyptian slavery, He took them on a journey into the desert and eventually through the desert. But whether His people were in Egypt, the desert, or the Promised Land, the goal of our God was always the same:

He was freeing them to know Him.

He was freeing them to worship Him.

He was freeing them to love Him.

He was freeing them to be with Him.

Just as He wants to free you and He wants to free me from our striving, from our burden, from the ache of not-enoughness.

Do you know this ache?

I've carried it as a gaping hole in my heart since childhood. A thirst I carried into all my relationships, into all my work, into all my thoughts. I thirsted to measure up. When I did, I drank it in and couldn't get enough. It's funny how drinking in the wrong things only makes you thirstier.

I carried the thirst into marriage. When Zac and I would have normal married-people fights, I would crumble, experiencing an extreme reaction, all because of a relationship that couldn't satisfy me. My frustrated determination to live up to my parents' expectations, to teachers' expectations, to coaches' expectations, to people's expectations, to Zac's expectations eventually moved to mistakenly thinking I could not measure up to God's expectations. So I began to avoid the only place where that thirst could be quenched.

It may be different for you, but I see the desperation in so many eyes. We can't go our entire lives with burdens we won't share; they are taking us down.

Jesus didn't come just so you would know about grace—or even so you would know about God. He came so that you would drink in grace and be filled with God. Emptying out whatever it is you fear that would keep Him from delighting in you somehow makes room for all of Him to come crashing in . . .

Cleansing you.

Filling you.

Freeing you.

Empowering you.

Jesus didn't come desperately needing something from us; He came to be with us.

Immanuel. God with us.

I need to stop here and be so clear because perhaps you don't know exactly why it is we do not have to measure up to God's perfect standard.

Jesus Christ, God's Son, did for us what we could never do for ourselves: He measured up. He was the perfect sacrifice. He is the only One to have ever satisfied all God asks to be in relationship with Him. And instead of keeping that for Himself, He trades places with us. He trades His enoughness for our scarcity and lack. He took on all of our sin and all of our not-enoughness, and put them to death when He was put to death on the cross. And for those of us who have named and turned from our sin and have trusted Him alone for salvation, we now not only measure up before a perfect God, but we are beloved by Him.

It is a story I do not ever get over.

We don't have to perform for a God who already adores us as His adopted children. I am not saying we turn apathetic and lazy, but I am saying we get to stop trying to impress God. God wants to be with us. And that reality pressed deep into us produces anything but apathy. Being wholly, relentlessly loved never makes someone apathetic. But it erases any need for earning gold stars.

Cooper thinks his stars matter to me, and sure, I am pleased when my children obey or succeed. But what he can't comprehend is that I am just as utterly smitten with him on his worst days as I am on his best ones. He has me. I may lose my temper, but that kid has woven his way into the deepest parts of me. He is my son, and his performance and achievements or lack thereof could never add to or strip one ounce of my love for him.

Perhaps intellectually you already know this about God's love. You know He loves you, but you have trouble experiencing His love, believing His love is really as steadfast as He says. Then take that disconnect, that doubt, straight to Him in prayer and open conversation and confession. It is when we get truly honest with God and ourselves that He can begin to heal and restore the holes in our hearts.

When we see ourselves the way God sees us, we don't have to strive.

Being near to God doesn't produce pressure or legalism; it produces worship.

FACING THE SCARY, BEAUTIFUL TRUTH

A couple years ago at the start of our second IF:Gathering, I stood in the dark at the back of the theater. I'd just delivered one of the shakiest talks of my life, barely getting through it. What few knew was why it was shaky.

In the ten days leading up to that moment, I'd endured a full-on assault.

It began with a rash that announced the arrival of shingles, followed by an unrelated infection. In the midst of my misery, I was still naively and stupidly shaking my fist at the devil, saying, "Bring it." Well, he apparently appreciated the challenge, and days before IF, I was on my bathroom floor throwing up from one of the worst pains I have ever felt. Let's just say it made me wish for labor and delivery. Nope, strike that. It made me wish for death.

A cyst had ruptured in my abdomen.

In the midst of all that came calls about a crisis within our organization, a crisis that propelled me into some of the most difficult leadership conversations I'd ever had—and trust me, I've had some doozies. So from my bed, in crazy pain and loaded with a lot of medication, I endured dozens of difficult calls. I wondered if our baby dream called IF might just die days before we even got to our second gathering.

But we finally made it through. I delivered my rough broken talk, still believing the lie that I had to hold this thing up and together, that I had to fight the dark cosmic forces coming at me.

Now here I stood in the back, hiding in the dark. Shelley Giglio came to stand beside me. She saw the fear. How could she not? It was all over me. She grabbed my trembling hand, and I said aloud the terrifying words that revealed my biggest insecurity, what I am so terribly afraid is true and everyone knows.

"I am not enough for this.

"I. Can. Not. Do. It."

And then one of my most treasured mentors confirmed my greatest insecurity. With a peaceful smile, Shelley delivered the devastating truth: "I know. And that's why God picked you, Jennie."

My deepest, darkest fear was true?

And no scary truth has ever set me more free.

Of course, I hated that she confirmed it. Because what I thought I wanted was my self-esteem puffed up. I wanted her to tell me I was enough. I wanted to be the best and to know that's why God picked me. I wanted to be especially gifted and smart and brave.

I want to be good enough to lead this thing. I want to be enough for God, for you. And that's my sin. Deep down, I want to be enough. I don't want to keep needing God.

I am realizing **it's not my curse that I believe I am not enough; it's my sin that I keep trying to be.**

All the while Jesus is saying, *I want to free you from your striving, free you from your doubt, free you from your pride that cares more about your achieving something than you receiving something.*

I am enough.

So you don't have to be.

Numbing Out

L ast night as I lay down to fall asleep, my thoughts chased down memories from the past few weeks:

- My four kids digging through their Christmas stockings and each laughing, disappointed that the bottom was full of oranges.
- Zac smiling over our "romantic" barbecue dinner with paper towel napkins and strangers sitting next to us at our picnic table, then saying spontaneously, "I'm really glad I married you."
- My sisters relentlessly making fun of me for days because I somehow managed to make our waiter spill a tray of fifteen drinks. Seriously. That is almost how many kids we have between us.

With my head on the pillow, I mentally scrambled to catch these moments and stuff them in deep. I thought if I could catch enough moments and tie them down and secure them somewhere inside, that life would mean more, that it would slow down, as if marking my days in some way made them count more, made me count more.

Because most days, I move through with no markers, no memories. I move through most days numb. I live my routine. I manage the chaos. I survive.

In the past three years one of my closest friends, Sarah Henry, had a massive stroke and my sister walked through a divorce. Meanwhile I felt overwhelmed by the demands of a quickly growing ministry, Cooper and my other growing kids requiring my attention, the haunting needs I couldn't meet around the globe, and just life and all its pressures. My backpack was getting unthinkably heavy. So rather than entrust the weight to God and people doing life with me, I would just lean that pack against a wall and watch seven seasons of *The West Wing*.

Surely this is not what following Jesus in this life is supposed to feel like? My greatest fear became missing the beautiful joy of a life God had given me. I was hustling for the people I love and for God, and yet in the chaos I was missing them.

It is not enough to simply acknowledge that Jesus is our enough; we need to be freed from our backpack existence quite regularly. We are missing our lives. Striving is stealing our joy, our moments. We are not meant to simply tick off the days until we go to heaven.

When we live trying to measure up on our own, one of two things happens:

1. We STRIVE.
2. We NUMB out.

Or we combine the two, and eventually we numb out because we get tired of striving.

Numbing and striving are two indicators that we are trying to find our worth in something other than Jesus. It reminds me of a high school classroom. You have the strivers, the straight-A students with their perfect homework and their hands raised, performing. In the back of the class are the slackers, who gave up a long time ago. They are checked out, watching the clock and waiting for class to be over. Maybe this has something to do with our personalities and bents. But I think each of us expresses these two gears of striving and numbing in unique ways. You may be a pleaser or an achiever, or maybe you are a rebel. But you and I both have the same needs: to be deeply known and unconditionally loved. Which means that, no matter how you express it, you, too, crave acceptance. Eventually we all get tired of our chronic thirst, and it feels simpler to check out than to face it.

Numb is easier than pain. Numb is easier than striving. The weight of sin or stress or hurt surrounds all of us, the burden and pain of failing to meet our own expectations, of not being the neighbors, managers, daughters, friends, spouses, or parents we wish we were. This is not who we thought we'd be, and we're tired of trying to change our reality.

Turning everything off through social media, busyness, six seasons of *Friday Night Lights,* alcohol, work, or even religious activity numbs us and helps us cope with all the heavy or hard things flooding us every day.

But numb is not living. Numb is sleepwalking through our one gift of a life.

One problem with being numb is that it is less detectable than sadness or anger or joy. People don't often even think about it except that usually, just under the surface, there is a nagging sense that something isn't right.

If I were to ask how you are doing, would you be able to answer the question?

How are you doing?

We have an autoresponder for this type of question.

"I'm good."

"I'm fine."

"Okay, I guess."

But how is your soul?

Are you truly fulfilled and happy?

That feels invasive and terrifying to answer. We proceed from one unchanging routine to the next, from our usual breakfast cereals to the Monday morning work meetings, errands, or carpool lines, the routes we drive to and from home and predictable recipes we cook for dinner, the recurring conflicts we mediate between our children, and even the order in which we wash our face, brush our teeth, and climb into our pajamas at the end of the day. For most of us, days are blurred into years or life stages, and the unique story lines playing out in our God-given lives become wearisome instead of our delight.

WHAT ARE WE MISSING?

The mundane parts of life aren't the enemy to God's movement; they are the soil for it. We dismiss ourselves and miss that we actually were created and equipped to be a part of the gorgeous, eternal story the God who adores us is building here.

We tend to segment our lives into silos.

We divide what we think is the spiritual from the practical.

We divide what we think is the important from the mundane.

We divide what we love to do from what we think we are supposed to do.

We divide our family and friendships from the mission of our lives.

We miss that God is mixed into every part of life and wants to entangle eternal story lines and encounters into our everyday activities and people. We're separating all the parts that are supposed to bleed together, and yes, they will make a mess, but God crafted this chaotic recipe of faith and fulfillment.

One day not long ago, I turned off my cell phone at 5:00 p.m. and observed as everyone stayed busy with homework or television or friends. At first, I would pick up my phone occasionally to check it, only to find out it was turned off. Then I remembered I was supposed to be watching my life.

I watched eight-year-old Coop bring me a book about Legos to read to him after he had crawled into my lap. I watched ten-year-old Caroline ask me to help her with math that in third grade is already outsmarting me. Fourteen-year-old Kate plopped herself up on the counter and told me stories about her day while I stirred chili. Sixteen-year-old Conner came downstairs and joined our conversation and set the table for me, after I asked him to of course.

I watched my life instead of my phone, and I loved my life.

Perhaps most of those things were happening on other days, but I wasn't intentional and present enough to catch the details and appreciate the gift of it all.

And, yes, God is in these ordinary moments, and He is also calling us to do wild and obedient things we could have never imagined. It isn't either/or, it is both/and. Sometimes we don't even know which are the big things and which are the small. **Heaven will tell the stories earth missed.**

Our identity must shift from helpless, striving, surviving, insignificant small humans to eternally loved, secure, confident, dangerous, empowered people on a clear, noble, eternal mission, who also happen to accomplish that as they are teachers, clerks, executives, janitors, mothers, and friends.

A Big Vision That Wakes Us Up

I believe we crave vision almost more than any other thing. Right up next to our deep thirst for love and relationships and acceptance is a need for a vision that inspires and ignites all our other cravings. Vision actually awakens us from numb stupors. Yes, we sometimes choose numbing as an alternative to striving unsuccessfully to accomplish big things. But a true, God-focused vision awakens us to something both greater and more attainable than what we've been chasing.

I have a crazy dream that every person who believes in the name of Jesus Christ on earth would unite under His name and love each other and God in a radical way such as the world has never seen in any generation before ours.

It's a big vision, and I am sure as you read these words you're tempted to glaze over because it's lofty or not helpful to your immediate need to pay your bills or find the right therapist for your child with autism or help your parent with cancer or help you meet a guy who may be marriage material. Or this vision simply doesn't help your sad heart that you don't even quite know why it is sad.

But I actually think a big vision could change all that. (Maybe not the meet-the-right-guy part.) When we have a clear, wild vision,

- we truly need each other and find relationships,
- we feel a part of something bigger than ourselves and find acceptance, and
- we recognize our need for God like never before, and we find His love in ways we never have before.

I keep coming back to the Bible, and the God of the Bible, because it is absolutely compelling and it satisfies that deep part of me that aches for purpose and vision and something bigger than myself. And if I am a fool for believing all these wild things and spending my entire life on Him, at least I am not the only fool.

This book, the Bible, is full of strivers and visionaries and everyday shepherds and salespeople.

- Paul made tents and preached and considered his entire life, the glory of it and the pain of it, an utter loss in comparison to knowing Jesus.
- Noah had a rebellious kid and built a boat that happened to save humanity.
- Abraham pulled his entire family into the desert and mostly just hung out there for his entire life. Yet God was fulfilling purposes that would extend for generations and even into eternity.
- David tended sheep in the middle of nowhere, and he happened to learn how to use a slingshot, which came in handy later.

- Joshua served alongside Moses, invisible, for years during which he developed faithfulness and faith that would lead a generation into the Promised Land.
- Ruth cared for her mother-in-law, gathered food, and found a good man. Then she raised her children and happened to be raising the ancestors of Jesus Christ.
- Nehemiah had a secular job for a pagan king but was in the exact place to help rebuild the wall of Jerusalem, protecting and bringing together God's people.
- Jesus was a carpenter, and His men were tax collectors and fishermen and single and parents and missionaries.

It is supposed to all blend together—our everyday roles and the story of eternity. But all too often we compartmentalize and miss it.

When Zac and I were in seminary in Dallas, the school offered symphony tickets to students at a very low cost. I had never been to the symphony. Truthfully, I'd never wanted to go to the symphony. Zac secured the tickets and surprised me on a date night. I wasn't sure I liked the surprise.

As we sat amid the awkward shuffling of people taking their seats with hushed whispers cluttering the silence, I regretted spending valuable babysitting dollars for this. Then a sole violin cut through the awkward stiff air. It was stunning, but still I wasn't moved.

Then the flutes joined. I relaxed a little.

Then every one of the nearly one hundred instruments flooded the room with sound. I fell apart. I leaned back and I tried to process it. Each string and each key and each note working in unison built a beauty I didn't even know existed.

You and I were built to enjoy the symphony God is always playing. We hear only a single seemingly random cymbal clash and a bleeding undertone of a cello. We miss the whole because the parts are all broken up and have lost their beauty.

Every story and human in the Bible—all were building one story they never could have imagined at the time. The symphony they were a part of led to the Son of God coming to earth to pull an entire people into eternity.

I suspect that when David was shearing sheep, he wasn't clear on that point.

Certainly Daniel, sitting down to his salad while others around him dined on steak, didn't know that he was paving the way for a carpenter who would one day sit down to eat with sinners and save us all.

When I read their stories, when I read God's story, I start to feel like an absolute fool if I spend even one day of my gift of life here numb, checked out, distracted.

You and I actually know what our mundane, eternal stories are leading toward: Jesus coming back and seizing His people and building a kingdom that won't end.

If we know all that we know, living on this side of Jesus's life and mission, if we know Him and are filled with His Spirit and called to this epic, gorgeous eternal story, how could we ever for even one minute check out?

But we do.

Because we forget the bigger symphony and story, we start to resent and even neglect the small, mundane parts of our lives. If we could realize the small parts are building heaven, maybe we wouldn't check out from them.

Jesus said, *Don't you know that whenever you feed someone hungry, or clothe someone naked, or give someone thirsty a drink, you are doing this for Me?*[1] The small things aren't only building eternity; we also find Jesus as we live them. Jesus is in the midst of each ordinary, messy, mundane moment. It is where we often meet with Him, as we build spreadsheets in our cubicles, as we drive carpools, as we share a meal with friends, as we do dishes. These are the places we dwell with Him.

Vision and rest and work and joy and Jesus and difficulty are meant to coexist. But too often, caught up in our own cycle of striving and numbing, we lose sight of the beauty and grand story unfolding.

MAKE THE WORLD GO AWAY

As the weightiness of the past few years caught up with me, it felt wrong to admit that my days felt dark, especially when I didn't exactly know why. So much of the weight came from things that were also blessings in our lives.

For months I mulled over the obvious culprits behind my struggle: spiritual attack so blatant at times I have laughed out loud at how obvious the devil can be, pressure to protect the purity of this "great work of God," the chaos of all the hard work mixed with four kids growing up at turbo speed and me feeling like I was missing it.

I remember one night in particular lying in bed and saying, *You know? If this is what it means to follow You, God, I don't know if I am up for this.*

I'd been in God's Word. I'd talked to friends. I'd prayed and prayed and prayed. I'd fasted, for crying out loud. I had done everything that I could think to do so that something would change, because the darkness was overwhelming me. But I was at a loss.

I looked at my life and saw this Barbie Dream Castle: an amazing husband, four healthy and mostly happy children, a beautiful church, a circle of kindred dear friends, a growing ministry using my gifts, reaching the world for Christ. Not only were all my basic needs met, but my above-and-beyond wishes and dreams too. And yet for some reason every day I was overwhelmed with this feeling that all I wanted to do was kick it in. Yep, an overwhelming desire to kick in the Barbie Dream Castle, and I did not know why.

Why couldn't I enjoy it? Why couldn't I find happiness? Where was it?

If I am honest, I wasn't miserable and feeling intense sadness; it was more that I had chosen to be numb.

I wasn't crying myself to sleep, more like falling asleep to *Gilmore Girls.* Thoughts that regularly crossed my mind:

I don't want to be with Jesus; I want to be with Netflix.

I don't want to be with my kids; I want to be taking a nap.

I don't want to connect deeply with friends; I want to connect deeply with my Barefoot Dreams robe and a gallon of Cookies 'n Cream Blue Bell.

Life had become so important and weighty, I was missing the happiness in all of it.

For so long, earlier in my life, I immaturely thought life was largely about finding my comfort and my happiness. Then as God moved me in deeper with Him, I saw rightly that life is really all about loving God and people wildly.

Happiness had become wrong, and suffering for God and people seemed only right. But my understandings of life and God were like an overly weighty pendulum, swinging dramatically from one conviction to the opposite.

My striving/numbing conundrum was in full swing when Zac and I received an invitation to spend a week at our friends' lodge, which sits adjacent to a Young Life camp called Malibu Club up in the middle of nowhere Canada.

As we approached our time at the lodge, coming to any understanding about the root of my unhappiness felt impossible, and coming to some big emotional life change at an actual Young Life camp felt cliché. My highest hopes were to laugh and make some memories with Zac and my friends. But here was the problem: at the lodge, where I was surrounded by a whole lot of happiness, my own unhappiness was impossible to escape or ignore.

I wanted my joy back.

I wanted my freedom back.

I wanted my feelings back.

I wanted my passion back.

I wanted my dreams back.

I wanted my life back!

I had seen God move in spectacular, miraculous ways, and I'd seen God move in quiet, behind-the-scenes ways that could only be His hand at work. I'd witnessed answers to prayer, such as loved ones being saved, individuals being freed from addiction, job offers coming through, ministries being launched, children finding new courage.

How could someone who has seen the power of our God move in so many ways ever be so checked out and so unhappy?

It terrified me, but it was happening. I was frozen inside, with no clue as to why or what to do with it, burdened with weights I thought I had signed up to carry because I trusted Jesus.

So after a few days in the camp, while on a walk to dinner with Zac, I admitted what I had been terrified to say out loud, scared even to admit in my head to myself: "I know something is terribly wrong in my soul. My life needs to change. I just don't know exactly how to change it."

When I talk to a lot of women, I hear the same hunger in their stories. When I meet you, I see it in your eyes:

You want your joy back.

You want your freedom back.

You want your feelings back.

You want your passion back.

You want your dreams back.

You want your life back!

One night after dinner I snuck away to spend some time with Jesus. It was as flatlined a time as I have ever known. I didn't cry. I didn't read. I sat there looking at the sky, asking God what to do with the weight I felt, with my miserably heavy, invisible pack. My soul was about to be resuscitated, but it wouldn't be in ways that I could have predicted. God brought me there because He was ready to radically shift the way we were doing life together. He wouldn't let me miss my life, He wouldn't let me miss His love, He wouldn't let me miss Him.

He came after me, and He is coming after you.

A fellow lodge guest stumbled up the path, seemingly lost. He was an older gentleman with silver hair and sincere eyes. I'd heard others around the camp refer to him as a wise counselor. A wise counselor. That is exactly what I seemed to need. Someone to diagnose me, someone to explain this heaviness that had invaded my life.

As he walked up, I said, "Sir, I know this is going to sound crazy, but I think I'm supposed to tell you my problems."

He laughed and sat down next to me. Over the course of the next hour and a half, the man listened patiently to every significant and insignificant thought about my life, the heaviness of my Barbie Dream Castle life and lack of enoughness. My absence of emotion turned quickly to fanatical emotion, and I found myself crying on this poor man's shoulder and wiping my eyes and snotty nose on his shirt.

I told him about my overwhelming urge to kick in the castle of accomplishment. I told him how desperately I wanted to hear God say, "Well done." I told him I was afraid of messing it all up. I told him about my constant not-enoughness. I told him my heart wasn't pure enough, I wasn't a good enough leader, God picked the wrong girl. I told him how much I wanted to please God.

He listened and smiled and nodded, and can you imagine what he said?

"Jennie, kick it in!"

What?

"Yes, kick in the castle. If this is God, you cannot mess it up and ruin it no matter how hard you try. And if it isn't from God, then you just did Him a favor."

My brain was spinning out as freedom and peace seeped into every part of me. I pictured myself kicking IF in . . . all the expectations, the pressures, the dreams realized. And I pictured it popping back up like one of those inflatable jumpy castle things.

He said words like:

"Jennie, God doesn't *need* you, He *loves* you."

"No wonder you are so tired, that is a lot to keep up."

"I'd rather be watching Netflix than be with Jesus, too, if I lived afraid of failing Jesus all the time."

"God couldn't care less about successes, failures, visions, disappointments. He will just use all of it, whatever means possible just to get to you, to be with *you*."

I laughed out loud at the absurdity of all the lies I'd been believing and the seemingly noble aspirations I had inflicted on myself to prove I was capable to lead such a thing. How silly to think I could manage this God movement. How arrogant to believe I could hold this thing up if my heart could only be pure enough.

I realized that night that I have been living a lot of my life *for* God instead of *with* God. And that is a lot of pressure on a girl.

That night, as near to heaven as I have ever felt, God whispered, *What if all you ever wanted, all the happy you have craved, just happens to be found in loving Me and people wildly?*

Of course that. Of course.

I knew it; I just didn't believe it. And it turns out there is a difference.

He whispered, *You know your soul is craving Me? Only Me. That is what you crave. That is life. That is peace. That is hope. That is joy.*

I pictured Jesus calling me to this great adventure but saying to me, *Jennie, come to Me, you who labor and are heavy laden, and I will give you rest. Take My yoke upon you, and learn from Me, for I am gentle and lowly in heart, and you will find rest for your soul. For My yoke is easy, and My burden is light.*[2]

Jennie, I want you to stop doing things for Me and start doing things with Me. We have some fields to plow and your eyes have been straight ahead, working and striving and pulling this heavy thing. Look next to you for one minute. Look over.

I look, and there's this enormous Ox beside me.

There I am, little me strapped in next to an enormous Ox, and it's God. He was always there. The reason I could rest wasn't because the job is easy, and it wasn't because I am capable of achieving it. It was only because I was strapped in next to GOD. He would do the work, and I could rest because He is so strong, so good, so kind.

He is saying, *There is Me and Me and Me and Me and you with Me—or you without Me.*

I was making this harder than it has to be.

You see, God has called us to His huge vision. He is calling us to go and make disciples of the world and to show people Jesus and to see people transformed. He has called us to feed the poor and bring hope to the sick and love our families through the hard days. He has called us to lives that set people free and to invite them into the family of God. While sometimes we miss the wonder because we daily live out our calling in mundane ways, He has called us to an exciting and noble and awesome task, and if you are not a part of it, I can promise that is one reason that you feel like you are missing something—because you are.

We can't make light of the vision, but we also cannot accomplish any of the purposes of God unless we do them with the power and the resources and the energy of God.

All of a sudden I knew what to do with my backpack. I would no longer strive under it or lean numbly against a wall with it while watching Netflix. I would hand it off to the Ox who had led me here and was with me and more than capable of carrying such weight, and I would start to enjoy the places we would go together. He was actually just waiting for me to see that He already had been carrying it all along.

Coming Up for Air

I almost died at summer camp when I was eleven.

We had all taken kayaks and canoes and miniature sailboats to a little island off the shore of the camp, where we stayed for a few days in tents. I always opt for things like showers. I am pro-showers. So I was eager to get back to the mainland. When it was time to load up, I grabbed three friends and we got a head start on our chosen watercraft, an itty-bitty plastic sailboat.

About halfway across, ominous dark clouds rolled in. Within minutes it was raining. So picture four eleven-year-olds in a sailboat in a decently wild storm. Panic was already our reality. I was in charge of the ropes that controlled our sail. The harder I pulled, the faster the boat went, and we were in it for speed. Given that I was eleven and knew next to nothing about sailing, the boat was all over the place. Before I knew it, the metal pole securing the sail knocked me into the water. The ropes causing the sail to tighten and speed the boat along were now wrapped around my neck.

I vividly remember the darkness of the water as the boat dragged me through it. My weight pulled the already tight sail even tighter. I was the thing making the boat go fast. I was the tension. The boat was choking me, and the controls to the boat were tied around my neck.

I would pull the ropes away from my neck long enough to swim up and take a breath, but I could not get untangled and the boat could not stop. The power of the wind was so strong that I could only get a breath for a second, and then I would have to go back under the dark water and be dragged along. I wasn't strong enough to pull the ropes off.

The boat was pulling me faster and faster, and I kept trying to come up for air.

I was as helpless as I have ever felt.

I could not save myself.

As a parent of four kids who attend camp now, I can't imagine what I would do if I were standing on the shore watching this happen to one of mine. Before I blacked out, a counselor who saw what was happening kayaked over and jumped in and untangled me.

Someone had to save me. I couldn't save myself.

And so it is with us.

Life is pulling us faster and faster, and we keep trying to come up for air. We are being dragged along by life, and add to that the enormous backpacks strapped to our backs . . .

We cannot do this ourselves. We have to be saved.

If you're exhausted from the struggle to prove yourself, you are not alone. This is the story we all find ourselves in.

This story has a villain. The villain scouts our lives and presses in at every crack he can find. He gets into our heads. His is the voice we hear saying, *You are not enough. You can't do it. You are losing.* Something about those words rings terribly true.

Happily, our story also has a hero. But the hero isn't you and it isn't me. We tend to want to be the heroes of our story. When there is a clear villain, every one of us wants to spring into action and save the day. The hero has all the resources, the hero has all the power, the hero has all the control.

Those who are being rescued have none of that.

They just have need. They are flailing in the water or lying crumpled on a closet floor, crying into a dirty T-shirt. They have anything but resources, power, or control.

I used to think the best ending to a dark and difficult story was to be the hero, but now I realize being rescued is actually the most freeing, beautiful resolution to a story.

LIVING INTO THE TRUTH

I am not enough. It is a terrifying phrase that goes through our heads on quite a regular basis about a plethora of things. Let me tell you a few of the stories I have heard just from my close circle of friends.

Bekah leads boot camps. As she leads neighbors and friends through workouts, she also has seen them through cancer battles and through difficult divorces. She regularly is given the opportunity to talk about Christ, but she wonders all the time if she is doing work that is important enough.

Laura has consistently been among the top salespeople at Noonday Collection, but she still comes home and wonders if her personality is outgoing enough to be in sales.

Sarah had a massive stroke and spends most of her days in rehabilitation, learning to speak and read and walk again. Yet she has found a way to communicate her worries that she is not a good enough mom to her three kids.

Jessie is in her sixties and divorced many years ago. Jessie glows with love for Jesus. Her kids are grown, so she has free time and recently came to a class on mentoring. But she never followed through. When I reached out to her about it, she said, "I didn't think anyone would want to be mentored by someone who has been divorced." Subtly saying, *I am not enough.*

I want to shake my darling friends. They are pouring out their lives in unique, obedient surrender to God, and yet they cannot see that the narrative they are believing is all wrong. And trust me, on a given day they've wanted to shake me, too, for believing the same lies.

We are so often dragged along in the darkness, unable to save ourselves from our thoughts and from our shame and from our mistakes. We try to slap self-esteem tactics on our fears, but they don't stick because, well . . . it's true. We are not enough.

It would be a terribly depressing thought—if it weren't followed by the most freeing truth in all of eternity.

God knew we would never be enough. So He became enough for us. Jesus is our enough.

Now before you glaze over like you are in sixth-grade Bible class, stop.

If memorizing that truth was enough to change us, we could end this thing right here. The problem with all of our souls is we think we know a truth, but we don't live like it.

Maybe you say you believe Jesus is enough, but then why are you not pulled up near to Him every chance you get? Why do we keep running to everything on earth except Him? Or why has your time with

Him become more of a chore than the thing that breathes life into your weary soul?

The truth that we are not enough and Jesus is enough isn't just good news on the day that God saves us. We need to preach that truth to ourselves and each other every day. We have been rescued from a life of striving today.

"Do you remember a time in your life when Jesus was near and real to you?"

My husband, Zac, recently asked me that question. He knew I was wrestling with trying to locate Jesus and find my way back to Him. He said, "Jennie, why don't you go home and pull back out your old college journals?" As I looked back at the abundance of chubby curly words I had scribbled in those years, I could picture my thick green Life Application Study Bible open amid the forest of sunflowers that was my bedspread and the decorating theme of my college freshman dorm room. That Bible, always by my bed, was thoroughly marked up. I'd scribbled my honest repentant heart to God on nearly every page.

In my journals I read about days on the campus bus, headed to class and praying for each person in that bus. Back then I prayed all the time. I needed God. I loved my local church. I couldn't wait for Sundays. Notes from church were scribbled throughout. I was so thirsty for God and for His truth and for His people. I wanted Him, I needed Him, and He was there.

Yes, these were the years when my eating disorder began to take hold of me, and as I headed out of college, it was threatening to strangle me. That season, like all of our lives, was a mix of joy and struggle and God and His work as I fought to find and establish my identity in this world.

But even during that time of internal conflict, there were scribbles of stories describing late-night conversations about spiritual things with people who weren't particularly spiritual. Our discussions were natural and easy and unforced. No doubt a tiny revival happened around us at the University of Arkansas in the nineties.

What was overwhelmingly present in my life in those days?

Constant prayer.

Constant confession.

A marked-up Bible.

An imperfect church I was so grateful for.

Journals and journals filled with stories of God moving.

Friends beside me who loved Jesus.

Friends beside me who needed Jesus.

And joy and peace and kindness and hope and fun and mission and risk and a full life.

While I know that going back to the simplicity of college days is not realistic or possible, I want to live an entire life full like this. I want to be full of Jesus to the point that He is pouring out of me.

So for the last year I have studied the life of Jesus through the book of John.

How did Jesus carry the biggest mission of all time without striving?

What did He believe about eternity and His Father and this life?

How did He move into and through suffering?

How did He live with all this incredible, enormous weight that should have been on His life?

Jesus lived with a deep security in His identity. He lived settled, content, dependent, with nothing to prove and with a clear goal of displaying His Father's love to every person He encountered.

Maybe you are thinking, *Sure, Jesus lived believing He was enough and had nothing to prove—because He was God!*

Yes. He is the only One who ever lived on the earth who was enough in Himself. But He was also fully man, and Jesus lived as an example of what it means to follow and walk with God. The Bible says, "Whoever claims to live in him must walk as Jesus did."[1] In other words, we are to be Christians (little Christs) in this life. We are called to live as He lived.

So we aren't going to focus simply on the words Jesus said while He was here; we are going to look at how He lived, His choices and His risks, His affections and His priorities, His passions and His frustrations.

Jesus was a shocking display of God during the time He lived on the earth. Actually, He still shocks us as we look at the way He lived, what He valued, and how He loved. He challenged the norms of His society, and He showed us how wrong we, as humans, can be about who God is and what He wants from us.

Colossians 1:15 says that Jesus Christ "is the image of the invisible God." Jesus was fully man and fully God, and He lived fully engaged with His whole heart, mind, body, emotions.

Fully connected to His Father and to the people around Him.

Fully present through the pain and the joy.

Fully aware of the need around Him and the part He was to play to meet it.

Fully satisfied in His identity and His place in His Father's story.

Fully confident in His Father's provision to accomplish His purpose.

This book is an exercise in finding Jesus and learning that we have nothing to prove, because we're living out of His abundance and letting it spill over into all the thirsty lives around us.

The point is to know God more and to give Him away.

Nothing is more dangerous, more compelling, more freeing, more radical, more real, more satisfying, more powerful than a person holding a smidgen of faith. A sincere faith in Jesus and all He wants to do around us wakes us up, rattles our lives, shifts every perspective, issues hope in pain, and ignites purpose.

So we begin our look at Jesus with John 1. The moment in history that John is trying to wrap words around? All of history had been building to it; all of eternity was building it.

> In the beginning was the Word, and the Word was with God, and the Word was God. He was in the beginning with God. All things were made through him, and without him was not any thing made that was made. In him was life, and the life was the light of men. The light shines in the darkness, and the darkness has not overcome it. . . .
>
> The true light, which gives light to everyone, was coming into the world. He was in the world, and the world was made through him, yet the world did not know him. He came to his own, and his own people did not receive him. But to all who did receive him, who believed in his name, he gave the right to become children of God, who were born, not of blood nor of the will of the flesh nor of the will of man, but of God.
>
> And the Word became flesh and dwelt among us, and we have seen his glory, glory as of the only Son from the Father, full of grace and truth.[2]

God became flesh . . .

and dwelt among us . . .

God with us. Jesus.

If you are used to hearing or reading this statement, let me just tell you: for people hearing that for the first time—that the God of the universe became a baby human—it's mind blowing. Mind blowing. God became flesh.

God became flesh and *dwelt* among us.

Another jaw-dropping truth. The word *dwelt* there, in the Greek, means "to pitch a tent." I don't know if I've heard a better summary of Jesus Christ than that. He pitched a tent with us. He came down from heaven and set up camp and said, *Hey! I am going to build a fire, and I want you to come hang out with Me and see what God is like, because I am God. You can know Me and I will know you. I'm going to come down from heaven and sit with you and dwell with you.*

If that doesn't somehow move your heart, you are officially too numb.

When we see Jesus, we see God. What He is like, how He would live, what He would do, what He wants from us—or better yet what God wants *for* us.

ALL BECAUSE OF HIM

Encountering Jesus in the past year has built this new way for me, this new path to knowing Him better and living in His strength and abundant grace and letting the Spirit work through me instead of striving.

But this new way actually is coming back to old things. **We come** back to the simple, common graces of what it means to walk with Jesus.

I have found this pattern in Jesus's life, one I had never fully seen before.

He says, *I am the Bread of Life.*

He is the Bread of Life. We are not.

He says, *I am the Light of the World.*

He is the Light. We are not.

He says, *I am the Door.*

He is the Door. We are not.

He says, *I am the Way, the Truth.*

We are not.

He is enough. We are not.

I've lived so thirsty because I thought I knew where the water was. I believed it was on the other side of that ever-moving thick black line of expectations that begged me to cross it, and to get there I'd have to muster up the necessary resources from within me. That is why I was so tired. I was trying to be bread and light and life and enough, and I couldn't ever seem to do it.

But what I thought was a great disappointment was actually the greatest mercy God has ever shown me. See, we rarely go to drink unless we are thirsty. To feel our thirst is one of God's greatest gifts to us. To recognize our need for God is the beginning of our finding Him.

He built our bodies to signal our thirst for water, and He built our souls to signal our thirst for living spiritual water.

"If anyone is thirsty, let him come to me and drink. Whoever believes in me, as the Scripture has said, streams of living water will flow from within him."[3] The original Greek phrase here indicates that these streams will flow "from his innermost being" or "out of his belly" or from the very depths of us. So Jesus is saying to all who are thirsty, *Come back to Me and I will keep satisfying you. And out of that life with Me, from the deepest parts of you, love will overflow and bring life to others.*

Each of the chapters to follow opens with a retelling of a scene from the gospel of John, stories that reveal how Jesus consistently moves toward the people who know they are not enough. Then He reminds them that they are not enough, but that He is. I'm convinced that our perspectives will shift as together we witness a pattern of Jesus telling us again and again that we are not enough, but He is more than enough.

He is enough, so we don't have to be. In fact, it is downright arrogant to keep trying to be. The reality is that He is the enough we could never be. Like He promised us in John 7, *If you are thirsty, come to me . . . I won't only quench your thirst; I will cause streams of water to pour in you and through you.* All we crave in abundance is in Jesus . . .

Because Jesus is enough, we can experience true fulfillment.

Because Jesus is enough, we can live connected with Him and others.

Because Jesus is enough, we can rest.

Because Jesus is enough, we can risk for His glory.

Because Jesus is enough, we can trade fear for hope.

Because Jesus is enough, we can embrace grace.

Because Jesus is enough, we can live out our true calling.

You can choose to live in these overflowing streams of His enoughness. Will you choose Him instead of living pulled along, missing your life, unable to take a deep breath?

We cannot save ourselves. But this story has a Hero.

Will you let Him save you?

If you don't catch anything else about why you never have to prove yourself, hear this: IT IS JESUS.

Jesus redeeming our past at the Cross, as the perfect sacrifice, clearing our name forever and making us right with God forever.

Jesus redeeming our present because He promises to use our worst moments and our best moments for His glory and our good. Every day we still make mistakes. The fact that you are fighting sin doesn't prove that you are not a Christian; if Christ were not in you, you wouldn't even care. He is in us and with us, helping fight our sin and redeeming all of it for His purposes. This process keeps us from living arrogant in success and keeps us from ever being defeated in failure. He holds us up and together every day.

Jesus redeeming our future. We have nothing to prove here because "here" is not our home. And in the home we are getting ready for, we won't be comparing our actions; we are simply going to lay every gift and work and joy all down at Jesus's feet. We have nothing to boast in.

You have nothing to prove, because you are forgiven, you are loved, you have a home.

This year we watched our oldest son become a man. Mid–football season Conner was asked to play starting quarterback, as a sophomore, in one of our biggest varsity games of the year. The older starter was injured. It was a lot of pressure, even for a boy who, not so long ago, wanted to be the real Spider-Man as his chosen profession.

The morning of the game, I dropped him off to meet the other players for a team breakfast. He opened the door and paused. He turned around and said, "Mom, I've never been so scared." Then—*bam!*—he slammed the door and stoically walked in to breakfast with all the other boys slipping into men.

I couldn't drive. I pulled over into a parking space and cried a bit (because tenth-grade football players maybe can't do that over breakfast tacos, but their moms can outside in the car!). Then I texted him—a seriously long text with all the words I wish I could have said before he closed the car door. As we embark on a journey into believing Jesus is enough for us, I thought maybe these words would be fitting for you today too:

> Son, God seems to be in the business of stretching us past our abilities, resources, and capacity. It is just past ourselves that we see more of Him and He is best seen through our lives.
>
> "Fear not, for I am with you; be not dismayed, for I am your God; I will strengthen you, I will help you, I will uphold you with my righteous right hand."[4]
>
> Conner, nearly everything you have ever done has been within your capacity. This may be what excites me most about this moment in your life: what is required of you is beyond your age, experience, and current ability.
>
> In my life, these have been the moments that have most built my faith in God. Because as you surrender and trust Him and jump into what scares you with all of yourself, you watch God strengthen you, help you, at times even carry you, and you don't remember what happened. That is my prayer for you: that you would experience how much God loves you, how much He wants to help you, how powerful it is to trust Him to do what is beyond your own resources.
>
> I love you and I am unthinkably proud of how you have submitted to your coaches and team this week. You have led them by serving them and working hard, and moving forward even though you feel weak and scared.
>
> "But he said to me, 'My grace is sufficient for you, for my power is made perfect in weakness.' Therefore I will boast all

the more gladly of my weaknesses, so that the power of Christ may rest upon me."[5]

I know you've asked me what it looks like to be humble . . . It looks like you this week.

Head down.

Working hard.

Being afraid.

Doing it anyway.

Thinking of your team more than yourself.

Needing God.

Knowing that when it goes well, it is because of God.

Knowing that when it goes terrible, it's okay because you have God.

He is in you, Conner. He is with you today and tonight, and we'll be there too.

And to you who feel afraid, broken, overwhelmed, inadequate, stretched beyond your capacities, God is about to get so big and dear to you too. Just wait . . .

Part 2

....

GOD'S STREAMS
OF ENOUGHNESS

5

No Longer Thirsty

I heard the men whispering. My father-in-law was visibly upset.

I couldn't imagine what could be wrong. We'd been celebrating my wedding for a perfect few days, and the party wasn't over. I couldn't wait to get settled into the business of starting our home and family, but I was savoring every second with our friends and family, dancing and eating and enjoying each other and all that Yahweh had done for us.

Across the crowd, my father-in-law and a small group of men began to pull in their wives, whispering and continually looking over at me. Their panic terrified me. I moved toward my mother. She was crying. When I got to her, she grabbed both of my hands, her eyes locked on mine. "There isn't enough. The wine is gone."

For months we'd been preparing for the biggest week of our lives. We knew it would be a stretch for our meager budget to provide for the many people who were traveling to celebrate with us. So many people loved and respected our families. We bought all that we could afford, and as families we prayed over the boxes of food and wine, begging, "God, please let it be enough."

We'd been so eager to get married, and now our families would be facing our greatest shame. I couldn't breathe. Our friends who'd come to celebrate us would begin to judge and shame us.

The first wave of the coming flood of embarrassment and guilt hit me.

I slipped away to a quiet place. I knelt on the dusty floor and begged our God once again, "Please spare us from this embarrassment."

Before I stood, I heard the shouting, and then I heard the words, "The. Very. Best. Wine."

Days later, the guests were gone, and we'd nearly finished cleaning up the remnants of the celebration. The enormous clay jars, normally reserved for ceremonial cleansing, still sat in our courtyard, mostly full of the finest wine any of us had ever drunk.

I noticed my father-in-law staring at them. It was obvious he was even more confused than I was. He called for the servants.

Two quickly darted around the corner, and he asked them to sit down. "Can you tell us what happened?"

They exchanged glances but neither spoke up. Finally one of them cleared his throat and said, "Sir, I don't know. When the wine was running out, you know we were all panicked. Shortly after I came to you, the woman Mary called for me. Then her son Jesus simply asked me to fill the cleansing jars with water. I did it."

I didn't understand. What was he saying? We all had heard that Jesus and Mary had been part of gathering the wine. I was impatient. "But where did the wine come from?"

"All I know is that I filled the jars with water, and when I drew from the water, it was dark-red wine. That is what I brought to the master of the feast."

We all stared at the dusty floor.

We had been rescued by our friend. We were spared embarrassment. We were grateful.

But water to wine. It's just not possible. I had often wandered into the vineyards near my childhood home to be alone and think and steal a grape or two. The workers in the field were sweaty as they pruned back dead branches and tried their best to not disturb the grapes. After a year of waiting, the ripe grapes were gently picked. Then they were cleaned and smashed and their juice poured into jars that would often sit untouched for years to produce the very best wine. I could think of no harder work, no more patient labor than winemaking. The sweat, the work, the resolve, the patience; I was familiar with all it took to create fine wine.

And yet Jesus spoke and water became fine wine? Who is this man? Who with a word could do what takes dozens of men with an abundance of resources many years?

My father-in-law finally spoke. He looked at the servant and said, "Bring me some more of that wine."

We all laughed, but I wasn't settled. Jesus. I hoped He and His men would visit again. I wanted to thank Him for saving our wedding. But even more, I longed to understand who He was.

The Stream of Fulfillment

The sun was setting as Cassie made her way toward the man in full dress uniform, eager to become his wife. Zac and I had been a part of Cassie's life since she was in high school. She'd been a fixture in our lives, someone our kids had long looked up to. We all had watched her grow from an insecure darling girl to a mature godly leader who had finally met her match in Geoff. My youngest daughter, Caroline, distributed flowers ahead of Cassie. Zac stood behind Geoff, delighted to perform the ceremony. And Kate, my oldest daughter, sat beside me, watching this dream of a wedding unfold. The perfect weather seemed to be God smiling down on two of His favorites.

Afterward, when we got in the car, twelve-year-old Kate looked at me and said, "Mom, I want a wedding just like Cassie's. And her dress? I loved her dress!" And just like that, I flashed back to my own twelve-year-old self, legs draped over Dad's recliner as we dreamed and hoped and pretended we knew something about the future.

I was keenly aware that this conversation could go on to shape Kate's hopes and dreams for her life. It also could define how she perceived our expectations for her.

I work in an office full of phenomenal single women, most of whom hope to be married one day. To a great extent, the answer to that desire is out of their control. **Many of the things we think we need to be happy are just beyond our grasp.** I wanted Kate to know, even at twelve, that no man and no dreamy wedding is necessary to complete her, to fulfill her.

So after the lighthearted dreaming based on the Pinterest wedding we'd just attended, I glanced over at her at a stoplight and said, "Kate, if God wills, I pray you marry a man who loves Jesus and helps you to love Him more. But if you do not ever meet that man and marry, I believe you are one hundred percent complete as a leader, as a friend, as a daughter, as a woman, as a Christ follower. God has tremendous plans for you, and those plans may include a husband and children. But even if that's not the case, you will contribute beautiful chapters to God's story here."

Kate smiled. The light turned green. I wondered what she would say next. I wondered if she would push back. Had she somehow picked up the subtle lie that she needed a husband to be valuable? Did she just assume she would meet the dream guy and get married?

Her next words: "Mom, of course I know that. I have big dreams either way."

Tears welled up at her confidence and assurance in who God had made her to be, with or without a partner. I prayed and still pray that the enemy would never steal the truth that she is enough with Jesus, even if she has nothing else on earth.

A THIRST FOR SATISFACTION

Marriage and family have become idols in our culture, especially in the church. In addition to these supposed must-haves of mature faith, to prove yourself a committed follower of Jesus you apparently also need to have a stable job in the right field, be registered for the proper political party, have the appropriate friends, and maintain a modest savings account. Unless, of course, you forsake it all and move to a third-world country on mission.

God forgive us for deciding what it should look like to follow Him, for suggesting that fulfillment comes more from the life we build here than in the life that waits for us with Him.

We are utterly sick from self-absorption. We've bought into the lie that the more we consume, the more satisfied we will be. Yet consuming more of this world only makes us thirstier.

Everyone is looking for excitement and a recipe to a full, rich life. We have a deep, built-in yearning for satisfaction. Somehow we miss that the most exciting, fulfilling rush of an experience comes in following the Spirit of God.

Following Jesus . . .

doesn't mean you have the prescribed 2.5 healthy children.

doesn't mean you won't live paycheck to paycheck.

doesn't mean you will get your dream job.

doesn't mean you will meet the person of your dreams.

But it does mean, even promise, you will be fulfilled. Jesus promises complete fulfillment. It just isn't found in the things the world prizes.

I believe you and I crave the beauty and joy and freedom that come from receiving our lives rather than consuming them. But we don't know how to make the shift. So we try to appease our craving by chasing mirages in the desert, reaching for illusions of water rather than water itself.

When I looked up the word *joy,* I was surprised by all of its synonyms: *wonder, delight, elation, satisfaction, fun, happiness.* I hate to say it, but these are not words I would use to describe you and me most of the time. Here is my fear: we have somehow come to believe that it is wrong to be happy. Maybe it's because we're too aware of the suffering of friends nearby or the suffering all over the world. Maybe it's because we're carrying the pressures of work and life. Maybe it seems that fun is an escape from responsibility rather than an attribute of people who know God.

I flash back to the urgency to please and obey God I had for several years and see now that it had strangled much of the wonder, delight, elation, satisfaction, and just plain fun out of my life. With life feeling more and more hectic and cluttered, my soul was so obviously unfulfilled. I had a lot of the things of God but not God Himself. The heaviness of my life began to cause me to miss the moments and people that are the best parts of my life. True fulfillment means we have the ability to live present in both positive and negative experiences and not miss either, yet I was bitterly aware that all of it seemed to be slipping through my hands.

Not only is God the creator of wonder, joy, satisfaction, and fun, but He also issues all of that with His sheer presence. But somehow as I surrendered to God, like a pendulum, I swung from "life is about my happiness" to "life is about suffering for Jesus." Initially, when Zac and I prayed, *Anything, God,* wonder and joy exploded as God initiated and inspired new adventures. But somehow those miraculous, obedient story lines became wearisome and noble tasks we were supposed to execute for Him.

And so the question before us is:

Does God want us to live fulfilled and happy?

Jesus lived with quiet, peaceful joy rooted in a deep, settled fulfillment, and He issued those over and over to the people near Him. Jesus had His mind fully set on the next life. He came from heaven and knew what awaits all of us there.

However, with heaven in clear sight, Jesus lived fully in this life, creating opportunities for the people around Him to see more of God. Turning water to wine as guests celebrated a wedding, eating unforgettable long meals with strangers and friends, celebrating the extravagance of perfume being poured out for Him here. Jesus created moments that those He loved could never forget. And He chose to enjoy the people around Him and the work He had here.

As I approached Jesus's life, I came with a heart wide open, seeking the answer to the question, *Jesus, why am I so unsatisfied?*

LET'S BEGIN WITH A PARTY

When I lean into the book of John to study Jesus's life, the very first miracle finds Jesus at a wedding party. I get such a kick out of this. I picture God in eternity past making plans for Jesus's time here on earth, and the Trinity decides, *You know, let's make Our first miracle creating wine at a wedding.* I will say that when I approached this scripture, it was in faith that there was more to this story than God likes a good party. Because I don't think that preaches very well or accurately. So what is it about this miracle? Why does Jesus start here?

Again and again Jesus showed up at everyday common occasions and turned them into symphonies. He didn't just teach with words; He often illustrated His hopes for us through unexpected metaphors. In this case He attends a wedding and explodes extravagance into an ordinary event. Water to unending incredible wine. This was a strategic message, not just a party trick.

Wine in the Bible is often used as a metaphor. In fact, it's used as one of the most significant metaphors for the most important event in history. Near the end of Jesus's life, at the final supper with His disciples, He poured wine and said of it, *This cup that is poured out for you is the new covenant in My blood. When you drink of it, remember Me. Every time you drink or eat, remember that My body was broken for you and My blood was spilled for you, all to fulfill a promise, to confirm a new covenant between God and you.*[1]

So what is the new covenant?

It is pretty awesome. The wine would be a symbol of the greatest news on earth.

> For this is the covenant that I will make with the house
> > of Israel
> > > after those days, declares the Lord:
> I will put my laws into their minds,
> > and write them on their hearts,
> and I will be their God,
> > and they shall be my people.

And they shall not teach, each one his neighbor

and each one his brother, saying, "Know the Lord,"

for they shall all know me,

from the least of them to the greatest.

For I will be merciful toward their iniquities,

and I will remember their sins no more.

In speaking of a new covenant, he makes the first one obsolete. And what is becoming obsolete and growing old is ready to vanish away.[2]

The death of Christ, remembered with wine, promises the opportunity to be near to our God, to be in relationship with Him, to know Him, and to receive His grace.

Forever the new wine would mean:

The end of our sin.

The end of measuring up.

The end of proving ourselves.

The beginning of what we were made for: nearness to God.

For generations humans had been trying to cleanse their lives and mistakes and dirt and sin. The fact that, at the wedding in Cana, Jesus had the servants fill the huge ceremonial cleansing jars with water highlights the ultimate goal of His life and death and resurrection: He would replace the inadequate religious rituals with the flowing promise of nearness to God.

The old cheap wine of measuring up and stale religion is gone. But the new wine answers our deepest craving—and it never runs out.

The nearness of Jesus is enough to infuse joy in the midst of everyday experiences. But why don't we live as if we believe that? Instead of hovering as near to Him as possible, we often chase the mirage of joy and then are surprised that we still feel empty. Jesus not only delivered wine; He delivered the best wine. I think often we go to Jesus for salvation but daily miss that Jesus is offering us the extravagant rich blessing of presence with Him. We walk past Him, settling for cheap boxed wine.

The Cheap Wine of Entertainment

We have gallons and gallons of the best wine, yet we keep drinking cheap wine. *Joy* is defined as "the emotion of great delight or happiness caused by something exceptionally good or satisfying." By contrast, the definition of *entertainment* is an "agreeable occupation for the mind; diversion; amusement."[3]

We were made for wonder, but we've settled for entertainment. God built us to crave true, fulfilling joy. But for many of us, that God-given craving for heart satisfaction has driven us past God Himself, who was meant to be the fulfillment of those desires, toward a drug that dulls the ache of dissatisfaction and disappointment but never truly fulfills us.

I have a new purse that still makes me a little happy when I look at it. It is okay if I spend some money on a purse—and I did spend a bit too much on it. But it's not necessarily a sin to spend too much on a new purse.

The sin is that I think it is going to satisfy some craving in me, apart from Jesus.

We've traded the wonder and satisfaction of a deep relationship with our Creator for Netflix, social media, and a new purse.

My friend Aaron Ivey, who leads worship at our church, writes incredible worship songs that move me. One of my favorites is called "Jesus Is Better." I want you to pause for a minute and think about that line:

Jesus is better.

Better than every single other pleasure on this earth.

Better than being in love.

Better than the comfort of a beautiful home.

Better than a month-long vacation on the beach.

Better than the most incredible meal.

Better than Nordstrom.

Better than being liked.

Better than your dream job.

Better than sex.

The psalmist says, one day with You, God, "is better than a thousand elsewhere."[4]

If you're truly honest with yourself, do you really believe that Jesus is better than anything else in the world? I think I want to believe that. I know I'm supposed to believe that. But on a daily basis I do not believe it, or at least I do not act like I believe this. I usually settle for a Starbucks run and scrolling through Facebook rather than time with Jesus. If I didn't believe the lie that these shallow, empty pursuits would satisfy me, I guarantee you I wouldn't keep exchanging mirages for Jesus.

So then I must believe there is joy in this life apart from Jesus. Oh, how I hate to admit it, but the evidence of that belief is that I keep getting surprised when this world and everything I run to in it does not satisfy me.

Do not be deceived or confused. Our joy, or our lack of it, is a direct result of where we most spend our time and thoughts and energy. And Jesus works completely backward from the world and the lies in it.

Your soul is most fulfilled in the small, quiet moments on bedroom floors where you pray or in comfy chairs where you read your Bible or in your car where you worship God with Hillsong turned up so loud you can't hear yourself singing. Your soul is more fulfilled by giving of yourself than by consuming. Jesus knows this, and He calls us to a backward way that happens to give us all we were hoping for.

Time with Jesus actually helps our wild souls be still and remember the incredible story we are part of. Time with Jesus causes us to feel secure in our identities. By listening to His voice, we recognize the lies that promise fulfillment elsewhere.

Do you want to know what you truly believe will satisfy you? Look at where you spend the most time.

The danger for us is not that we would enjoy the cheap wine on earth but that we would grow addicted to it. I fear many of our distractions are becoming flat-out addictions. We as a generation are addicted to entertainment, amusement, agreeable diversions, Netflix, social media, shopping, alcohol, food, careers, vacations, even relationships. For me at this very moment, it is *The West Wing,* as in seven seasons. Count them. Seven! Before that, *Gilmore Girls.*

What if abundant joy, bliss, wonder, pleasure are ours, and we just kept missing them for fleeting entertainment?

Jesus offers all we crave and more. He says to us, *You know your cheap wine runs out every single time, doesn't it? Have you noticed this? It keeps running out and it doesn't even taste good and yet you keep drinking it. I'll tell you what. You're tired. You're weary. I'm going to give you something that will never run out, that will never quit satisfying you. In fact, in comparison to the cheap wine you've been drinking, it will be the greatest thing you have ever tasted. Do you want that?*

Yes. Every one of us says yes. But do we want it bad enough to turn from immediate amusing diversions and be in the quiet alone with Jesus?

There are no spiritual helicopters out of the desert, just the old, common, gorgeous, lingering roads paved by our forefathers in faith and designed by God.

Knees on the ground.

Words formed to God in prayer.

Bibles marked up and worn out.

Hours spent with the only One who satisfies and delights our souls.

We want to do things for God without spending time with God. It is an epidemic in the church, and we wonder why we are so empty and unhappy. God built us for Himself, and all our attempts to manage life apart from intimacy with Him only further expose our ache for Him.

Jesus began His public ministry with an image of where it would end: His blood poured out for us.

Wine means joy.

Wine means satisfaction.

Wine means I will measure up for you.

Wine means I am enough for you.

Wine means that you no longer have to be addicted to the empty diversions of this world.

Wine means you are free.

So what does it look like in our everyday lives?

Jesus was pretty clear what to do with anything that causes us to sin: *Cut it off; cut it out.*[5]

Cancel Netflix.

Cut up your credit card.

Put down your phone.

Be with your people.

Pick up your Bible.

Get on your knees.

Don't miss the better wine. Linger with the only One who fills your weary, empty soul.

DO WE WANT TO WANT GOD MORE?

A few weeks ago out of conviction of all the ways I have chosen cheap wine instead of Jesus, I turned off my phone for twenty-four hours. I made sure the school had a good number in case of an emergency. I let work know I would be offline for a day, and after all that, I settled into it. Sort of.

At first it felt freeing to have nothing vying for my attention. But it wasn't even an hour before I noticed myself reaching for my phone. Similar to the alcoholic who reaches for a drink, I subconsciously reached for my addiction.

But when I would remember and set it back down, every time I felt His peace flood me. My mind felt clearer. I thought, *You know what? I get to be present. I get to enjoy this day and the wonder of just being still with Jesus.* No Instagramming it, no assembling notes for my next talk, no brilliant observations. Just Jesus and me and time. My soul filled up and my view of my life moved from duty to the wonder of seeing mundane moments from Jesus's perspective.

The discipline and gift of fasting is that it reveals where our affections have become entangled. When you reach for the thing you have become addicted to and it's not there, you remember, *God, You're better. Jesus, You are better.*

In this past year, Zac and I have been trying to cut back on all the things we tend to reach for to satisfy our longings, things like Netflix and sleep and food. Don't worry; we do eat! But for nourishment rather than comfort. I do sleep, but most mornings I am up very early.

Let me tell you what has happened as I have chosen God over this world: He is so much better and more dear to me. The apathy and numbness that for months had lulled me into a place where I craved comfort more than a massive movement of His Spirit; it shifted. Now I find myself waking up and craving God again. I feel compassion for my neighbors instead of the characters of *Parenthood.* Now, don't hear me say those things are evil! Dang it, I will eat cheeseburgers and watch all the new episodes of *Gilmore Girls.* Don't you worry.

But I've learned that freedom comes in fasting from the things we have accidentally started to put our hope in.

Because here's the thing: I want to want God more. I want to reach for Him in prayer as soon as my eyes open each morning, instead of picking up my phone. When I face disappointment, I want to crave His comfort rather than Cookies 'n Cream Blue Bell. I want to enjoy His love for me rather than trying to get it from people who can never satisfy me.

This world's cheap wine always runs dry. Always leaves us unsatisfied.

We search for a miraculous answer to the ache we can't shake. But we already have it. We already have Him.

Close your eyes. He is real and alive and with you right now, the One who with His Word pours extravagant, rich, unending floods of wonder into the voids of your soul.

From Him flows everything you crave. Do you believe it?

Now I should be clear on this one important point. You are going to ache; you are going to groan for more.[6] Scripture says this is true, especially for those of us who have gotten a taste of God. We won't be completely, everlastingly full until we are home in the place we were made for, in heaven with God. The meal that the wine and bread point to is the one we'll enjoy when we are finally with our God, eating at the marriage supper of the Lamb. That is when all your senses will be satisfied and all your cravings will be fulfilled.

We need to stop trying to make earth be heaven. C. S. Lewis wrote, "If I find in myself a desire which no experience in this world can satisfy, the most probable explanation is that I was made for another world."[7] We were. In the meantime, Jesus gives us a taste of the ultimate fulfillment to come. May that taste compel us to draw daily nearer to the only One who will ever fulfill our souls.

EXPERIENCE GUIDE

BE STILL

> And the LORD will guide you continually
> and satisfy your desire in scorched
> places
> and make your bones strong;
> and you shall be like a watered garden,
> like a spring of water,
> whose waters do not fail.
>
> *Isaiah 58:11*

One way we taste and see more of Him is through intentionally living as Jesus did, creating experiences to drink Him in and enjoy Him more. In the midst of distracting cheap diversions, intentional experiences help facilitate time with Him.

There is a war. We have to fight to help each other remember that there is joy in laying down what the world says is going to give us life. The goal of this book isn't to create new experiences; this is an exercise in finding Jesus and learning what it means for Him to be our enough. The point is to know God more and to give Him away.

Experiences are not the goal, just the means to the above ends.

Nothing shifts our perspective more than meditating and dwelling on God's Word. For each chapter I've included a passage for you to spend time with. Let it soak in, live with it, do not move quickly past it.

STEP INTO THE STREAM

When you look at your life and how you spend your time, what is the most tempting addiction for you? Name your cheap wine. How is Jesus better?

WADE IN DEEPER

Plan one hour and be with Jesus in a new way.

- Arrange time to be alone.

- Pick a new, unique, inspiring location.

- Take your Bible and journal and a pen.

- Turn off your phone.

- Be.

QUENCH
YOUR
THIRST

Take a Technology Fast. I know this may feel painful, but this Sunday turn it all off. Zero screens. Come up with some creative ways to use the time.

I find it most helpful to make a plan for the day, to intentionally schedule activities that will help me enjoy the time and recharge. You can plan time with friends, get outside, enjoy church, be with Jesus, take a nap, enjoy your family.

THE OVERFLOW

Right now, pick up your phone and text one friend a passage of Scripture she needs to be filled up.

No Longer Lonely

Based on John 4

The dust plumed up beneath my feet as I walked. Even the relentless rays of the midday sun felt markedly more comfortable than the stares of the other women when I came for water in the morning. Each time I passed the few other people braving the heat, I stared at the cracked, parched ground. I have disciplined my eyes to not dart up.

I was relieved to find myself alone at the well. I could draw my water in peace and hurry back home.

I was so thirsty.

As I lowered a leather bucket into the well, a man's voice surprised me. "Give me a drink." I looked over to see a man who was visibly tired and dirty from a long journey. He was Jewish, and we both knew He shouldn't be talking to me, a Samaritan and a woman.

When I asked why He spoke to me, my candor drew a kind, boyish grin across His face. "If you knew who I was, you would be asking Me for water. Whoever drinks My water, he will never be thirsty again."

I was intrigued. My daily trips to the well were saturated with dread, with the fear of hurtful whispers or yet again being pushed away. Many times the women would immediately leave when I arrived. Their rejection stung. Every once in a while I could blend in unnoticed among the gathered crowd and listen to them laugh and share stories about their children playing nearby. Even then the loneliness stirred up in my chest, threatening to choke me.

But I had to come. I had to get water. I carried it home to drink and cook and wash in, but it didn't ever make me feel clean. Those women, they were clean. Their lives were honorable and managed and tidy.

I wanted His water so I would no longer have to come to the well and risk the shame.

But instead of giving me the water, He asked about my husband. It felt mean, as if He knew what I ached for and was holding out.

My jar wasn't yet full, but I wanted to escape. I answered short: "Sir, I do not have a husband." I was bothered by how dry my mouth was. If I wasn't so thirsty, I could run.

"I know."

What did He know? He sat down on the rock nearest to me, searching for my eyes that were trying to avoid Him. How could He know? He is not from here.

He kindly and quietly said, "You have had five husbands, and the man you are with now, he is not your husband."

I was caught. Everything I'd been running from, everything I'd been hiding from, He was throwing in my face. No one knew about the other husbands. They were offended enough by my current living arrangement. I had been on the run, concealing my even more sordid past. How did He know?

"You are obviously a prophet, so maybe You can answer something for me. Where are we supposed to worship? Everyone seems to have differing opinions about this."

My back was to Him as He spoke. "I know there have been all kinds of rules in place for how to worship and love God, but everything is about to change."

There was something about the way He said it, the authority and kindness of His words even though He knew all the shameful things I was doing my best to hide. I just had a feeling He was the One we had all been waiting for. The thought terrified me. *Messiah, here now and talking to me?*

"Woman, I am He. The time has come."

I knew. I knew Yahweh had brought the Messiah to me—me!—and He knew the worst of my mistakes and yet He didn't despise me. I was undone by His love and the hope in His eyes. Everything shifted in me. I wanted everyone to meet Him. I didn't care if they saw me; I didn't care if they knew. In fact, I wanted them to know. I wanted them to know that our Savior was here and He cared about me. If He wanted someone like me, then surely they would all feel wanted too.

Men came over the hill, men who seemed to know Him. I left the well, left my water jars behind, and ran toward the city. Outside the market I could see the group of women with their children. I stopped. *How will they know I am serious? How will they believe me?*

And then I did it, the most freeing brilliantly foolish thing in my life: I led with everything I had been hiding.

The Stream of Connection

We recently got away for a night with some good friends in the hill country of Texas.

Honestly it was one of those nights that if you looked at my Instagram feed you would have been jealous. I'm just telling you. It was a dream getaway. These are some of my very favorite, long-time friends. We've shared over ten years of friendship and life together with these couples, and it was just easy. You probably know how difficult it can be to make couple friends as a couple. It's just tricky. You have to like the woman and he has to like the guy, and they have to like both of you, and then your schedules have to align, and yada, yada, yada. Anyway, we have couple friends, and we took a dream getaway sans the billion children we had produced between us all.

We sat at dinner till the restaurant closed. The waiter had set in front of us one of the most elaborate Pinterest-worthy cheese boards with fifteen types of sliced meats and gorgeous cheeses spread out. Zac's and my very favorite food on earth, next to queso and chips, is a great cheese board.

Heaven will contain a lot of cheese.

I think we actually prefer crackers and cheese to chips and queso (and all the Texans just clutched their chests), because it isn't as easy to scarf down. You slow down and talk and eat and look in people's eyes.

We ate and told the stories we rarely tell about nothing important. We snorted from laughing too hard at things like how Jesse lets Janet boss him around and how obvious it is that Jesse loves it. Then we quickly transitioned to tears over Julie's sadness that she can't have more biological kids because of her weak heart.

We all left feeling known, feeling seen, feeling connected, feeling less alone. I remember wondering why we didn't do slow time like this together more often.

As humans, we simultaneously crave connection and resist it.

The *New York Times* recently posted an article titled "To Fall in Love with Anyone, Do This." Like everyone else who read the title, I had to know what "this" was that could cause any two random people to fall in love. The article was based on a study conducted by Dr. Arthur Aron, who successfully caused two complete strangers to fall in love.[1]

The two strangers sat across from each other and asked each other a series of thirty-six questions that started with basic things like whom you'd most like to share dinner with and then gradually increased into more intimate questions like "For what in your life do you feel most grateful?" and "When did you last cry in front of another person?"

At the end of the thirty-six questions, the two strangers were to stare into each other's eyes for four minutes.

Have you ever tried to stare into someone's eyes for four whole minutes?

It is no small thing to stare into someone's soul for four minutes and all the while allow that person to stare into yours. It exposes you to feel seen like that. I think the risk usually proves too much. Most people look away. Connection is like that. Most people move away when it comes too close.

But we are not intended to live alone, to be isolated.

In the deepest part of us sits an enormous desire to connect. We crave intimate connection more than nearly any other thing, yet I would venture to say most of us feel a constant twinge of loneliness.

People surround us. We still miss each other. We can be sitting in the same room or driving in a car together and miss opportunities to really see each other, to really hear each other. We quickly move on like this and miss Jesus too. Loneliness can have a strange power over us. It tricks us into believing we are the only ones who are lonely. So we stifle the desire to share our most constant nagging fears and insecurities, while nearly every other human walking around does the same.

Recently a good friend handed me a book called *Becoming Human*. Jean Vanier wrote in it,

> I discovered the terrible feeling of chaos that comes from extreme loneliness. . . .
>
> We all have this drive to do things that will be seen by others as valuable, things that make us feel good about ourselves and give us a sense of being alive. We only become aware of loneliness at times when we cannot perform or when imagination seems to fail us.
>
> Loneliness can appear as a faint dis-ease, an inner dissatisfaction, a restlessness in the heart. . . .
>
> When people are physically well, performing creatively, successful in their lives, loneliness seems absent. But I believe that loneliness is something essential to human nature; it can only be covered over, it can never actually go away. . . .
>
> Loneliness in one form is, in fact, essential to our humanity. . . .

> Loneliness is the fundamental force that urges mystics to
> a deeper union with God. . . .
> Loneliness, then, can be a force for good.[2]

He basically says, *I don't care what your Instagram says or how many friends you have on Facebook. Every human being is lonely.*

And something about that is terrible, and something about that is comforting.

CALLED OUT OF HIDING

As much as I adored our getaway to west Texas, a surprising thing happened. The day after we came home from the Instagram-worthy trip, I woke up, and guess what I felt?

Lonely.

One day after I had just done the thing I so needed, I so craved, I woke up lonely. It wasn't because I missed them. It was because I had accidentally been thinking that the perfect getaway with the perfect people and a lot of cheese was supposed to fill my soul.

Somewhere I'd believed, *If we take this trip together, it'll be a memory maker. We will bond, we will have deep talks—everything I am craving. It will be amazing.*

And you know what? It was. It was all the things that I hoped that it would be.

But it still did not fill my soul.

Here's what I believe is happening: We are so lonely and we do not feel known; we do not feel understood. We do not feel connected to people in a really deep way because we are expecting them to fill something that only God can fill.

So, in our pursuit of deep connection, we have to recognize that we can often look to good things like community, authenticity, confession to take the place of connecting with Jesus. Loneliness is meant to be an invitation to draw closer to God. But our tendency is to try frantically first to meet that need with people, to prove to ourselves that we are lovable and funny and worthy of attention.

We are made for dependency on God. We were built for that. Because God is invisible we put our neediness on people, and that becomes unhealthy one hundred percent of the time. It's called codependency. If we connect with people and we don't connect with God, we end up asking people to be our enough. People will always eventually disappoint you. Don't be surprised. They aren't enough either.

Only God has the resources and ability to exhaustively meet your needs. Yes, we also were designed to need human relationships, but they can never be enjoyed if we're using them to replace the ultimate relationship. When we begin to find our deepest, most fundamental needs met in God, then we will go from using people to meet our needs to enjoying people despite the ways they disappoint us.

Community is meant to point us to Jesus, not replace Him.

Until we make that shift in our expectations, we continually go back into hiding because it's too painful to be known. But we give the illusion of sharing ourselves, a little like how the woman at the well said, "I have no husband"—telling a little of the truth, but not enough to reveal her brokenness.

And while you and I may not be hiding from women around the

well anymore, we often are hiding from being truly known. We post a version of our lives on social media and we share a version over coffee, but does anyone really know us?

Who knows that you lost your mind on your kids last week?

Who knows that you haven't talked to your dad in a year because of hurt?

Who knows you had an abortion in college?

Who knows you are sad?

Who knows you are lonely?

I am learning there is a difference between vulnerability and transparency. *Vulnerability* is the edited disclosure of personal feelings or parts of ourselves. *Transparency* is exposing the unedited, unfiltered, unflattering parts of our souls. I will be vulnerable with you in these pages, but let's be fair: it is an edited version of a selected sample of my worst thoughts and moments. Vulnerability is precious and useful and can serve great purposes, and it's as far as we need to go with most acquaintances and for sure as far as we should go for Facebook. But transparency is necessary with our closest people and especially with God. It's the only way we can truly be known. But it's a scary thought that sends us into hiding.

Our new hiding places include things like Instagram posts, a cute outfit from Anthropologie, obedient kids, an organized home, a meaningful job. But no matter what we arrange on the outside, we can't hide our eyes. Eyes reveal so much about our souls, and you know what I see when I look into the eyes of people I meet, people like you who are trying to do and be their best?

I see thirst.

What are we thirsty for?

The woman at the well was so thirsty.

She was thirsty to be seen.

She was thirsty to be loved.

She was thirsty to be right with people and God.

She was thirsty to be whole.

I think of how thirsty she must have been, waiting till midday to collect her water, wishing she didn't have to go, wishing she didn't need anything, wishing that she didn't have to come out of hiding.

We all wish we didn't need things outside of ourselves. We try to prove we don't need anyone. We take pride in going it alone, in making it through a rough week without seeking help. We may barely realize it, but we all are doing that.

This quote from C. S. Lewis helps explain why:

To love at all is to be vulnerable. Love anything, and your heart will certainly be wrung and possibly be broken. If you want to make sure of keeping it intact, you must give your heart to no one. . . . Wrap it carefully round with hobbies and little luxuries; avoid all entanglements; lock it up safe in the casket or coffin of your selfishness. But in that casket—safe, dark, motionless, airless—it will change. It will not be broken; it will become unbreakable, impenetrable, irredeemable.[3]

To love is to be vulnerable. Yet just as God built us to need water and food every few hours, we are built to never be self-sufficient. Our needs and our thirst eventually bring us out of hiding. Then the water we choose to drink will determine whether we return to hiding or discover how to enjoy our lives again, to enjoy people and relationship again, to enjoy Him again.

Jesus calls us out of hiding.

Jesus calls us to taste the living water that wells up and sets free and washes and restores.

Jesus says, *Let Me be your enough. You will be filled and you will be known and you will be free.*

And our enemy pushes us back into hiding so we cannot enjoy God and our people and eventually our lives. It is very difficult to even want to be fully engaged and present if we don't like ourselves and our lives. There are so many possible reasons that you might not like your life—hurt, regret, burnout, demands, conflict. Something about an encounter with Jesus is enough to change all that.

But first we have to come out. Like the woman at the well, we have to risk exposure.

Jesus met her at the well when she risked coming out of hiding. Then He exposed her shame in the middle of the day, and it could have been the meanest thing. Unless He actually had the answer to her biggest problem.

───

Maya was born and raised in India. She grew up in a good family and married a man her parents believed to be good and respectable. The wedding was a beautiful occasion, and her mother cried tears of joy.

Just days later Maya was being physically abused. Over time she suffered a broken neck, cracked spine, broken teeth and jawbone, and more. With her theater background, she was good at masking her grief and fear, but there was no peace, sleep, or security in her life. She started to experience blackouts. At first they were minutes, and then the gaps stretched into longer chunks of time.

One day, her abuser handed her the phone and said, "Call your dad. Tell him all that I'm doing to you." She begged her husband not to make her reveal her shame. She knew it would kill her parents to know of her pain. When her father answered, she later said, it was "the darkest moment of my life."

At that moment, she decided to run away. She managed to flee to Mumbai with few clothes and little money. To support herself, she would do street theater with street kids. Local traffickers who abused and exploited the kids thought Maya's teaching was interfering with their business. One day these men beat her.

She fled again.

The blackouts continued, and she ended up in a wheelchair, totally broken in body and spirit. She couldn't speak and she couldn't stop drooling. From her perspective, "Every shred of dignity left was lost." Eventually, she was reunited with her family, and they helped Maya to heal in many ways.

Today, Maya uses notes to speak. She's lost the sharp memory of a theater performer who could memorize all her lines. But when she speaks, she speaks of the One who knew her, who saw her, who loved her through every one of those dark days.

"My testimony is this," she says. "It was God, it is God, it will always be God all the while. Like you and everyone else sitting in this room, I wanted it to be simple. I wanted a normal life. I just wanted to be happy. Don't you want to be happy?"

Then she says, "Maybe God didn't want something normal for me.

Yes, it was a terrible story, but He's using the story that I am still struggling to be proud of to bring me to a place where I'm rescuing slaves from bondage."

Now Maya leads a team with International Justice Mission, the world's largest international antislavery organization. They work in a nation where 11.1 million people are enslaved, and Maya and her colleagues have freed more than ten thousand people in their country alone.

She bravely shared her story at IF:Gathering in 2016, where she said, "Ten thousand names and faces I may have never known or seen if my life had been totally normal and going perfectly well. Ten thousand individual human beings with stories of pain turned into hope."

To see her share with boldness on that stage was breathtaking. "Be that story, sisters. Let not that shame from the past restrain you. Go—go with joy, with confidence; go boldly with courage. And all the pain that held you back and held you there from not doing things. Go with a spirit of love and compassion and righteous anger against injustice. Just show up. Go."

———

Sometimes we think that Jesus is mean and unloving when He calls us out of hiding, when He exposes our flaws and brokenness and pain. But He calls us to set us free.

THE TABLE WE WANT

Nothing hijacks identity like fear. Fear speaks a dark narrative over our lives, over who we think we are. Fear tells us that we are defined by our worst mistakes rather than by our God or that we are defined by our image rather than by the image of the One who died for us.

Satan loves a man alone. If he can isolate you, he can make you believe whatever he wants.

Satan wants you shut down and living in his lies, believing you have to hide, believing you are not enough. He wants you focused on yourself and on your problems and on your sin, not fighting for the glory of God and fighting for souls. He wants you living in fear in this world rather than looking forward to an eternity that is for sure coming. So he will distract you with Netflix.

Downton Abbey, to be exact.

You know one of the fascinating things about *Downton Abbey*? The family doesn't go downstairs very often, and the servants don't go up except to serve. They certainly don't sit on the upstairs furniture. In the social hierarchy of the time, there was a dividing wall between the rich and the poor, those who were worthy and those who were not.

Our God came to take away the walls dividing family from servants. Our God says, *Guess what? You don't stay downstairs in the servants' quarters. Come upstairs and be part of My family and enjoy the riches and goodness of life I give to My children.*

This is your worth, this is your value, this is who you are. For eternity. No circumstance, no person, no mistake, no lie in your own head can steal it. It is true. You can believe the lies of the enemy that keep you fearful and hiding in the shadows, but it will not for one second shift what is true.

Our identity is secure. We are part of the family, but you and I too often hesitate to go upstairs and enjoy it. We stay downstairs in hiding.

We know in heaven we will be with God, at His table and enjoying Him and all He has for us.

But for goodness' sake, if we can go upstairs today and have a great meal and enjoy the gracious Downton lifestyle, I'd like to do that!

You are a child of God, adopted by the King, made to be—are you ready for this?—a coheir with Christ. Crazy, right? A coheir. Whatever Jesus Christ gets in heaven is our inheritance too. Amazing. This is our identity. Don't you know God is looking at us saying, *You are in My family. You are My kid. Why on earth are you hiding in the basement?*

When we hide, we diminish ourselves, we diminish our worth, we diminish our belief in God.

Maybe you believe that you are invited to the big table upstairs, but fear and suffering and pressure and shame block your path up the stairwell. I know it can feel complicated. But like the woman at the well, we don't have to let our circumstances keep us trapped in hiding.

Nothing changed that day for the woman at the well. Her circumstances were the same. Her shame should have been the same. Nothing changed. Except that everything changed. Because she had a new story. Her identity shifted at the well. Because *Jesus.*

The woman at the well entered a bigger narrative. She was no longer defined by her sin and weakness. God was defining her. She had nothing to prove. At the well Jesus said, in essence, *I came here to get you, adulterer. To get you, sinner. To get you, the most broken in the city. The one who is hiding. I came for you. You will tell the city about Me. I pick you to announce salvation to this city.*

The Father is seeking such people to worship Him, and I pick you.

She hears this and then she does something unthinkable.

She runs to everyone she was hiding from. She doesn't just run to them; she runs telling them about her sin! *I think the Messiah is here, and He knew my sin.* She leads with everything she has always tried to hide.

Is she crazy?

Or is she changed? Or is she free? See, the reason we hide is because we don't know what it feels like to live wholly forgiven. We've never known what it means to truly enjoy our lives, to run into a crowd with no shame, no fear, no guilt, no proving ourselves, no performance. Just us. With the amazing news of a Savior who happens to change lives.

He arrests us with His forgiveness and His grace, and He absolutely sets us free. He does not need us to perform. He is not here for a show. We just get to run with Him. It doesn't make sense and it's kind of messy—but it's wild and fun and what we are meant to do when the Spirit is filling us with everything our souls have craved.

Being known is what happens when you realize you are already known and, because of Jesus, you are already accepted. **You don't have to keep searching for what you already have.** The living water that eternally quenches our souls is filling us up. In fact, Jesus says it's not just filling you; it's welling up in you and pouring out of you. The living water floods in when we embrace our identity as children of God. The living water floods in and pours out when we have nothing left to prove and nothing left to hide. God is here, and we now run in freedom and share the worst of our lives because we are forgiven and new.

Just look what it did for the woman at the well:

She went from shame and hiding to being fully known and accepted.

She went from avoiding people to engaging everyone around her.

She went from thirsting for someone or something to fill her to being completely satisfied.

She went from wasting her life on sin to fulfilling her God-given purposes.

She went from embarrassed to overflowing with joy.

A Sweet and Wild Freedom

Sudden drastic change. It still happens today.

Not long after I returned from my perspective-shifting experience at the lodge in Canada, I was surprised to receive a phone call. It was someone I respected and liked, but when I answered the phone, I immediately was greeted with her extreme disapproval.

I sat paralyzed, braced for my typical spiral into panic. But something was different. I was okay.

I'd let go of striving and measuring up and performing.

And I'd embraced my inadequacy and sin. I'd embraced Jesus's overwhelming grace.

Something had changed. The usual adrenaline rush to turn someone's disapproval around didn't kick in. As she called me arrogant and unwise, it felt like a fist landing deep in my gut. Each punch had its turn, and each time I collected myself and felt a strange peace and resolve.

I calmly replied, "I know. You are right. I am arrogant and often unwise. And I am so sorry. Will you forgive me for the hurt I have caused you?"

This was a sweet and wild freedom flowing out of my intimate connection to God.

No defense.

No hiding.

No shame.

No running.

Yep. I am a disaster. I am caught and I am okay because I am forgiven. Today, I am closer to that friend than I was before that call. It is a counterintuitive move to put it all out there, but we are already caught. God knows we are prone to wander, and most days we know it too. How fun to not live trying to cover it up anymore. In fact, it is usually in the dirt of all that makes us human that the deepest, best parts of life and hope take root.

A sudden, drastic, awesome change.

The end of pretending and protecting.

The beginning of life-giving connection.

It reminds me of an episode of *Friends* when Phoebe calls out her friends' flaws. She says that Monica is high maintenance and Rachel is a pushover. They get mad and go to lunch without her in retaliation. Later, they approach Phoebe. Rachel says, "We are very sorry to tell you this, but you, Phoebe, are flaky." Monica says, "Hah!" But instead of defending herself, Phoebe throws back her head and laughs. She says, "That's true. I am flaky."

It is so refreshingly backwards to admit our weakness, rather than defend and cover it.

It is terrifying to be caught in our brokenness. But more terrifying than being caught is being alone and in the dark with all of our pride intact. Healing and wholeness are found only when we step into the rushing stream of forgiveness, of intimacy, of connection.

Step into the water.

EXPERIENCE GUIDE

BE STILL

When I fall, I shall rise;

when I sit in darkness,

    the LORD will be a light to me.

I will bear the indignation of the LORD

    because I have sinned against him,

until he pleads my cause

    and executes judgment for me.

He will bring me out to the light.

Micah 7:8–9

It's time to get caught because it's time you live free! It is terrifying, but Jesus's grace and freedom are waiting on the other side.

We all live with a deep need to be fully known and fully loved. No one does that perfectly on earth, but if we never risk being vulnerable, we will never get close to being known and truly loved. Risk it!

STEP INTO
THE STREAM

What is the thing you are hiding? You may feel like there really is nothing too big, but all of us are hiding away sin, most often from ourselves. Ask God to show you any impure motive or sin that you may not be aware of.

WADE IN DEEPER

Even more terrifying is confessing this to someone else. But it's part of getting free. Share the sin you are hiding with a trustworthy person, someone gracious and safe. Remember you are not alone. Around the world thousands of women are doing this too.

QUENCH YOUR THIRST

Gather some friends, safe people who have proven their love for you over time, and build a fire in a fire pit.

As you sit around the fire, share your story—all the parts, including the messy ones. Tell them you want them to know the mistakes you've made and the grace you are now experiencing. See what happens. I bet you will be around that fire for a while, and I bet your honesty will start a ripple effect, giving others permission to share their sin. I'm praying for all of you as you bravely go here.

THE OVERFLOW

Write a thank-you note to a friend who has shared vulnerably with you, and tell that friend how it impacted you.

7

No Longer Tired

Based on John 6

The sun was brutal. After days of walking and preaching and healing, we were exhausted and stopped to rest on a mountainside. We could soon see that a large crowd was following us.

Honestly, I was having doubts about continuing with Jesus. I couldn't deny that He was unlike any rabbi I had seen. For one thing, no other rabbi would have considered taking on the lot Jesus had chosen as His disciples. Our unlikely gang of fishermen, tax collectors, tradesmen, and misfits didn't exactly seem like religious material.

That was part of the reason for my doubt. I'd left behind everything that was comfortable, everything familiar and that I knew how to do well. Out on the road with Jesus, it always felt like I didn't have what I needed for the task at hand. I like to be in control. I like to have what I need. I like to be the expert. I like knowing what to expect.

My wandering thoughts were interrupted when Jesus looked at me and asked a question. I froze. He obviously was testing me. Thousands of people were heading toward us, and Jesus wanted to feed them? *Is He joking? He can't be serious.*

But He was.

And He was looking at me for a response. I couldn't breathe. I searched His eyes but found no hint of what to do. I searched the surroundings. There were no nearby markets or homes, and even if there were, we had very little money. It was impossible. I couldn't figure out what Jesus wanted from me. The rabbi often taught us truths by asking us questions, always surprising us and shifting the way we think and live. I couldn't begin to guess what truth He now had in mind.

"Jesus," I said at last, "it would take nearly a year's wages to feed these people."

He smiled and nodded and looked around to see if anyone else had the answer He was obviously looking for.

I couldn't help laughing when someone laid a few fish and loaves in front of Him. But Jesus asked us to have the crowd divide and be seated. We hustled around, unsure of what to expect. After everyone had sat down in the grass, Jesus broke the food into baskets and closed His eyes and thanked the Father for what was about to happen.

When He lifted his head, we began passing around the baskets of food.

We never came to the end of the food, and people just kept eating as the baskets continued coming around. After everyone had eaten as much as they wanted, we collected the leftovers. There we stood, holding twelve baskets overflowing with bread.

It was too much. Following this man made my every rational thought seem like foolishness. He lived aware of a world I barely believed existed. A world where everything we need is available in abundance and a loving Father is ready to pour it out to us as we do His work here.

I was tired of seeing only what was in front of my eyes. I wanted to see what Jesus sees. I wanted to stop wasting time in worry. I wanted to rest the way He rests. As I stared down at the baskets, I knew this was His way of helping us do just that.

The Stream of Rest

One day, exhausted from teaching the crowd, Jesus and His men got on a boat and a violent storm kicked up. Jesus was asleep as the wind and rain threatened to capsize the boat. While the disciples panicked, Jesus slept peacefully.[1] In all my study of Jesus, I can't find that He ever worried. Certainly, He was concerned about the people He loved and issues of the day, and as He faced death, He was afraid. But Jesus never wasted energy on doubt and worry. Jesus's spirit was gentle, unrattled, quiet within Him whether He was facing death or five thousand people who needed something from Him.

So many times the disciples were overwhelmed, but Jesus was at peace.

What did He know that they didn't, that we don't?

That day on the hillside, Jesus said to Philip, "How are we going to feed them?" According to John, He said this to test the disciple.[2] I've read the story of Jesus feeding the five thousand many times and heard it in Sunday school. But until my recent study of Jesus, I never really noticed that He was testing Philip. He wanted to shift the disciples' perspective about what it means to lead and love people. I think we would've failed the test, most of us.

I wholly identify with the disciples in their exhausted panic and worry. At times I've lugged around an awful lot of anxious, obsessive concerns tucked in my heavy backpack, and not just the big, heavy issues like suffering and leadership. Every morning of my life, I wake up to a lot of people coming up the hill, straight toward me, wanting Honey Nut Cheerios, lunches packed, and a morning snack, and then they come home after school with all their friends, who can eat through a Costco run in 5.7 seconds, and then it is time to think about dinner.

Whether it's physical mouths to feed or the pressure of deeply wanting to give Jesus to people, I don't seem to ever escape people flat needing things from me. Do you relate?

I want to ask you a question:

Are you tired?

Are you physically tired? Spiritually? Emotionally? Maybe all of those?

I want you to pick just one. Where are you the most tired?

Got it? Why are you tired?

I think we are all tired. And I don't think it always has to be this way. Often the truth of God, the immensity of His resources and strength, never occurs to us.

Here are the familiar questions that brought the disciples to this day and bring us to this point in our pilgrimage.

Am I enough?

Is there enough?

Is God enough?

Like the disciple Philip, we often stand paralyzed because we look at our lives and we fear there isn't enough.

Are we supposed to be this tired and defeated?

What has God put inside you to do for Him, and what would hold you back from that? What holds you back from putting this book down and absolutely going crazy obeying God no matter what He says? All in. What holds you back?

What is the voice in your head? What do you hear? Name it.

Is it rejection? Fear of failure? Disappointment? Inadequacy? Are you weary from trying to resolve all that? God isn't waiting for you to resolve it. He wants to move through these very weaknesses.

Because God is enough and has enough, we can rest.

This is counterintuitive. The world tells you the way to be confident is to believe in yourself. So we keep pushing forward in our resources to prove we have what it takes. But Christians know that the road to confidence and peace is believing in Jesus and what He provides.

An Impossible Hope

Go over to my Instagram and prepare to fall in love with my amazing kids. Scroll down. My youngest son, Cooper, is there—way too many pictures of him. Everyone thinks I like him more than my other kids because he's on my Instagram more than the others, but he is the one who always lets me take his picture.

Cooper was abandoned as a young baby and never knew his parents. Due to some complications in my son's paperwork, he was never matched with a family throughout toddlerhood. He became the oldest child in the orphanage by the time we came to get him. So that means that every one of Cooper's friends, in the nearly four years that he was there, was adopted while he was not. Cooper watched as a mom and dad came to pick every single friend he had. But no one came for him.

One day after he was finally home I asked, "Did you think we ever would come?"

His answer shocked me, "I knew you were gonna come, Mama."

So why would a four-year-old boy believe that he was going to be adopted? Coop didn't have a reason to hope for that. Nobody had told him, "You will be adopted." Or looked him in the eyes and said, "Your mom and dad are coming." They never told him he had a mom and dad until the day we were in the building. The minute that he met us was the minute after he found out he had a mom and dad. And yet it was as if he was just waiting for us, as if he knew we were coming and now we were here.

You'd better believe we had a lot of answering to do for the next few years as to why we had not come a little bit sooner. I always tell him, "Dude, I would've swum the ocean if that would have been enough to get you." He doesn't have much patience when I try to explain governments and paperwork.

The stories about my son in the orphanage for those four years he waited are legendary. Every visitor to the orphanage we've ever met remembers him. They tell us he was joyful and wild and smart. He even shared his occasional treats from Westerners with the younger kids. He broke up fights. He was a leader. The kid was epic.

He watched every friend he made get a family, while he continued waiting. Why was he joyful?

Coop had hope. He had a vision. He had a picture of a mom and dad picking up little boys on the other side of the blue door that guarded his orphan home. He'd seen a truck drive off with his friends into a world with a mom and dad and sisters and brothers. He didn't even know what a mom and dad were except that they bring you toys and juice and new shoes (he is really into shoes) and they take you away in a car that he had always wanted to ride in. Somehow that vision, that glimpse, that hope was enough while he waited.

He thought, *I bet that's going to happen to me one day.* Why wouldn't it?

If you and I could hold on to a clear vision and hope of a secure home and a God coming for us, I believe it would rest and still our fearful self-protective hearts.

Why do we struggle to believe that Jesus has come for us?

Why do we keep checking out with distractions and addictions?

Why do we hold back from all that God wants from us?

Even if we are doing some of it, why do our hearts so often feel discouraged and downtrodden, worn thin? Why, if we really believe that heaven is coming and it's not that far away?

If you look back at the three stories we have read about Jesus, you'll see a clear theme emerging. This theme sang hope into my weary soul as I desperately came to Jesus for a new way to do this life. Here is what He shouted to me from the pages of Scripture:

I go overboard for My people, My kingdom.

The wine. Go back to the wine. Did you see how I told you how big the jars were? I gave you exactly the size of the jars, exactly the number of gallons they could hold to show you that they would never, ever run out.

The woman at the well. She went to fill up her jar, to take a drink of water. I was clear: "I have water that will never run out. You will never be thirsty if you drink the water that I have." Abundance. Plenty.

The fish and loaves. I knew how many people there were and how much they would eat, and I made sure each one of My twelve disciples would leave holding a full basket to show them, to show you, I work in abundance.

You are enough and you have enough BECAUSE I AM ENOUGH.

This is how our God works, but we have been functioning in a scarcity mentality. Rather than trusting in His abundance, we try to be enough and get enough as if there isn't enough. And we are exhausted from trying to do all this on our own.

NOT ABOUT US

I have functioned believing that there is not enough. Feeling urgent because there is not enough time, anxious because the work is too big and there is not enough help, troubled that I am not doing enough, fretting that there may not be enough money, worried there is not enough space for what I want to create, and then if I do create it, that it is not good enough to be worthy of that space.

Maybe you have a God-given dream, and you look around and you see other people doing something similar and that shuts you down. You will get to see God work crazy miracles out of your life if you stop looking side to side and instead consider the good things that are right in front of you. But we look side to side and say, "Someone is already doing it; my dream is taken."

God must be thinking, *Are you kidding? Do you see the planet? There are about seven billion people. The world is very large. There is room for all of you, if I have called you to it. There is need in the world. Go for it! I actually have enough favor, gifts, talents for you to each accomplish the purposes I have laid out for you before time.*

Jesus wanted His people, He wanted us, to shift the way we view our lives and to shift our view of the way God moves and works. So He began the feeding of the five thousand with a test. He wanted to expose the limits of the disciples' faith and then bust through those limits to leave the ones full of doubt holding the leftovers of His extravagant more than enough.

In eternity past God planned, *I will make exactly enough food for how many bites every single one of these humans is going to eat, and then I will have exactly twelve baskets full when they're all done.*

That is an impressive miracle. Can you imagine the guys standing there, each holding his overflowing basket? Don't you know they must have been all looking at each other saying, "Daaaaang."

Their perspective shifted from what they didn't have to all that God did have.

God had a message for the disciples as they stood there with the overflowing baskets: With Christ all things are possible. *When you try to solve human problems with human resources in your human strength, there will never be enough. However, if you would like to follow Me and work with Me, I will meet the deepest needs around you and in you and through you with unending resources in supernatural, all-powerful strength.*

So what then is holding back God's Spirit from moving through us in miraculous ways?

I know what it was for me. Fear. I refused to sacrifice the idol of people's opinions. I was so afraid of the invisible thoughts of people.

Last night I sat with a friend who is wrestling through the tension of the call on her life and what people will think if she risks it and obeys. And her fear is that she would appear self-promoting. Oh, I get that! That was mine too. So I did nothing.

As if what God was calling us to had anything to do with us. As if our reputation mattered enough to sit on our gifts, training, and dreams that could actually help people and make God known to this world.

I think of Moses, when God asked him to be a part of setting His people free. God said, *My people are in bondage, and I want to set them free and take them to the land flowing with milk and honey.*

And all Moses heard was, "Me? You want me?" Then Moses and God went round and round about how inadequate he felt. But God's plan was never about Moses. God said He would accomplish the work. God alone would set free His people suffering in bondage.[3]

I'm not writing about this because I've seen this problem in everyone else; I've seen this unbelief in myself. I have seen this self-focused fear in myself today.

I texted Zac as I left to write today and said, "I don't know if I'm even good at this or if I should be doing this. I'm leaving my babies and I'm going to write about Jesus and I don't even know if I'm adequate to the task."

I texted this to him—*today.*

And as he often does he reminded me, "Jennie, this isn't about you. This isn't for you. God will accomplish *His* work to set *His* people free."

Like Moses, we begin to believe that since we are not adequate, then we shouldn't do what God has called us to. And we limit the work of God through us because we think it is all about us, our abilities, our resources.

But it is never about us. It is always about hungry people in bondage whom God wants to set free.

WHAT IS HOLDING YOU BACK?

Consider those things that are holding you back—the things you say you don't have enough of. Is it not enough talent? Money? Time? Space? Creativity? Personality? Need?

Now, I want you to picture the streets in heaven. I want you to picture streets as far as you can see and every street is full of warehouses as far as you can see.

I just want you to picture all that God has and all that He wants to do.

Then you land in heaven with Him. He looks you in the eyes and says, *I wanted to go crazy through you. I wanted to change your neighborhood, your city. And you kept going up to your room and watching Netflix.*

You say, "I wasn't enough. I wasn't gifted enough to accomplish that dream, God."

He says, *Come here. You see that road? Can you see the end of it? No? That is My road and all those warehouses have every gift. And on the road up there, those are the endless warehouses with money. And that one there was full of more vision than you could imagine, all Mine that I wanted to pour out through you.*

For all that I ever prepared for you to accomplish, I was also waiting to equip you with every single thing you needed to do it.

"But you know my past. I made so many mistakes. I messed up over and over again. You didn't even want me to talk about You."

He says, *Let Me show you something. Meet My Son. Look at His hands. You know why He went through that? To set you free. So that you could set others free. You were so forgiven, I especially wanted you talking about Me.*

Our God, He is waiting to pour out of us and pour into the world, but we stop Him. We think that He is limited. We think that He only picks special people and special things to appoint or bless. I'm going to tell you a secret: there are no special people. Ouch, right? You may be crushed right now, because you grew up thinking that you were a very special little snowflake.

But the truth is, you are just as human and jacked up as the next person, and given a different set of circumstances we could all be in jail.

We aren't alone in wanting to be special. This isn't just our generation; our ego-induced striving is quite a theme actually, spanning humanity's history since creation. Look back at the first humans: Why did Eve and Adam sin? Why did they eat the one thing God said not to eat? Because they wanted to be like God. They wanted to be special. Fast-forward to their kids, Cain and Abel. Cain kills Abel. Why? Because he's jealous of his brother. Next up, the first civilization of people build a big tower because they are trying to make a name for themselves.

This is a theme from the very beginning.

We fall right in line with all of history, all the humans. We want to be great and we want to be special. So we spend our whole lives trying to prove we're more special than the next person and using God to do it sometimes. We want miracles in our lives, but we want them our way, on our time, in our strength, and for our glory. So we force our will for our lives and often do it in the name of God.

And He says, *Nope, that's not how I work. In fact, you become noth-*

ing so that I can become everything, and I will do great things through you.

We make God and pleasing Him so complicated. But soon after Jesus feeds the five thousand, people are asking Him, "What must we do to please God?"

You know what He says: *The work of the kingdom is to believe in the One God has sent.*[4] You don't need a special anointing. You already have one. You are a child of God and filled with His Spirit.

Do you want to know why we are so tired?

Because we don't believe God. There is no remedy for your striving apart from finding your identity in Christ. He is your enough, and the degree to which you believe that is the degree to which you will stop striving, stop performing, stop trying to prove yourself.

I love this verse in Isaiah: "In returning and rest you shall be saved; in quietness and in trust shall be your strength."[5] It is in our letting go and in our trust that He rescues us. Yet we are striving and we are working so hard for God.

Guess what the person being rescued has to do? Trust the Rescuer and cooperate with the process. You and I don't need to be the heroes who save the world. We just get to be part of the story of the greatest Hero of all time. Which is good news, because being the hero is a lot of pressure and a lot of dadgum work.

You can rest because you know God is the One rescuing you and others around you. If God has rescued us, who can possibly get to us or steal us from Him? We rest.

We are not God's slaves. We are God's kids, the ones He sent His Son to rescue. He adores us, and He wants to move into the darkness with us. He wants to feed the hungry people who are coming up the hill. But as long as we are striving and trying to do it ourselves and trying to round up enough of our own resources to take care of the problem, we will keep being tired and cranky and resentful.

The beautiful alternative is to believe that our God moves in miraculous ways. We get to sit back and pray to Him and break the bread we have been given and watch Him meet needs—in abundance. We can trust Him with our people and surrender to Him our ways and plans and glory. And we can love Him because He is awesome and be with Him because there is nowhere better on earth than to be with our good, loving Father.

We get to trade striving for rest. We get to trade striving for confidence—not confidence in ourselves but in the power of a sturdy, heroic God, eager to rescue.

Do you know what God often uses to help us see our own inadequacies?

Need.

I think of the inadequacy I felt when we met our Cooper in Rwanda. He had health issues and we didn't speak his language and I've never felt more inadequate for a task. But he had no other parents in the world. He was in a third-world orphanage with a distended belly. I was in. I wasn't adequate, but how could I walk away? I would become more aware of my need for God in the coming months than in all the years of my life prior.

That's how we practice rest and trust: when we see a great need in front of us, we get over ourselves and fall on our knees, asking God to help us meet it. Oh, how we need to get over ourselves.

One reason I've never until now publicly shared about the eating disorder I struggled with as a young adult is that I still hate how self-consumed I became. I always was thinking about the next meal. I always was thinking about what I would or wouldn't eat. I always was thinking about myself and how I was not enough. Part of the sickness of our fight with enoughness is that it shifts our eyes from need to us. It shifts our eyes from people to us. It shifts our eyes from God to us.

Healing began for me when the need of another human came into the struggle. While I knew there was a massive problem and many friends worried there was a problem, I became really good at not showing how obsessive I had become. While Zac likely noticed I was very conscious about what I ate, I don't think he knew I had an eating disorder. The gift and freedom of God started when I found out that Zac and I were accidentally pregnant with our first child.

With a growing child inside me, I knew I needed to eat and to care for this baby. The transition of loving and caring for another human more than myself shifted my values and my priorities, took my eyes off myself. I wasn't healed overnight, but it was the beginning of my healing physically and emotionally.

When we hang out on the Internet instead of in our neighborhoods, when we look through magazines instead of into people's eyes, when we dwell on our own problems instead of the problems in our communities, we will always feel inadequate and shut down. We begin to feel like there are so many people doing cool things that we are not needed. But in the real world none of those cool people live on your street, none of them are loving your neighbors. God wants to do that through you.

So take the first step toward the dream God put in you. Take that first, risky, shaky step in obedience. When you do and God comes through, you'll laugh and want to take another one. Call the neighbor you've been wanting to love better, sign up for the art class in your community, tell your friend about the small-business idea you have been toying with, e-mail the adoption agency. Take one step.

YOU HAVE HIM AND HE HAS YOU

Seeing need and knowing only God can meet it causes us to run full of confidence, which means we can rest rather than strive. When Jesus promises us rest, He almost always is talking about *soul rest*. It's why most of the ways we try to rest actually make our insides more chaotic. TV, sleep, Facebook—all fall short because nothing but Jesus can bring rest to the chaos inside us. Through finding our identity in Him, confidence streams into our souls and empowers us to move creatively and intentionally through this life and somehow rest and enjoy it as we go about epic, eternal, world-changing, supernatural work!

Our confidence comes from believing God can do anything, then stepping back and letting Him.

We are trying to do the work of God without God.

Let's start doing things *with* God instead of *for* God.

Today He is saying, *Just ask Me. You are for Me? You are building My kingdom? Just ask. I am for you. You don't need to worry.*

Do you know that God has never *not* delivered? Goodness, He is good and always gives us enough. But usually it is our day's portion, our daily bread with a little thrown on top for good measure and to grow our faith. Tomorrow, the crowds will be hungry again. Each day brings new needs, new challenges, new problems, and every day He opens warehouses of bread. There is more than enough, but God wants us to keep coming to Him for it.

———

Coop has been home now for long enough to quit wondering and worrying if we are going to send him back to Africa, though that came up quite a bit in the beginning. Now he lies in bed and worries about things like his lacrosse game tomorrow.

He worries about whether his team will lose. He worries that he won't play well.

As he worries aloud before we pray together, you know what is running through my head? *I have you.*

He worries he won't have all his gear for the game. And I tell him . . .

You know what? Every piece of that gear is going to be there ready for you. You know why? Because I have you.

Then he worries he will lose some of his gear.

You know what, buddy? Your name is on every piece of that gear. You know why? Because I have you.

Then he worries no one will be there to cheer for him.

Hey, you know what? I'm going to sit and watch you, and I'm gonna cheer for you. Dad will be there and your sisters and your brother.

And guess what? We are going to get Sonic afterward, whether you win or lose. Because I have you.

Because I love you. I adore you and I am going to take care of you.

We are all so afraid there won't be enough, but we have a God who has us. When the disciples woke Jesus in the midst of the storm they feared would take their lives, guess what He did? He didn't chastise them; He told the storm to stop. He has us.

Sometimes the streams of living water Jesus promised us are calm and refresh us as we sit with Jesus. Sometimes the water is rushing and becomes a resource to give away to a thirsty world. The thing about Christ is that you know His streams will never run dry.

I pray you would catch a glimpse of a God who adores you, who wants to be in the mess with you, who will never leave you, who is for you, who has all you need, even—no, especially—on the very worst days. I pray that you would rest by the water and because of the water. I pray that you wouldn't just rest in your eternal provision as a part of God's family but you would rest in the everyday provision He is already dishing out everywhere you look.

He has you. He may even take you out for Sonic after the game.

EXPERIENCE GUIDE

BE STILL

Now to him who is able to do far more
abundantly than all that we ask or think,
according to the power at work within
us, to him be glory in the church and in
Christ Jesus throughout all generations,
forever and ever. Amen.

Ephesians 3:20–21

Imagine what could happen if you actually rested in the provision and goodness of God. Just like I have Cooper and I am meeting his needs, God has us and has incredible plans for our lives. What a waste if we get to heaven and realize all these years here could have been spent trusting God's abundance rather than fearing He wouldn't provide.

STEP INTO THE STREAM

- On a scale from 1 to 10, how worried are you today?

- Name what you are most worried about right now.

WADE IN DEEPER

Dream a little. What would you do if nothing was holding you back?

- Tell one person about the dream.

- Commit to pray for the dream.

- Identify and take one step toward that dream.

QUENCH YOUR THIRST

Invite a woman who loves Jesus and is older than you to lunch. During your conversation, ask her these questions:

- How have you seen Jesus be faithful in your life?

- When has God provided in abundance even though you doubted He could?

- What is one thing you would tell your younger self?

THE OVERFLOW

Next time you are with a good friend, invite her to share a dream with you. Ask, "What would you do for God or others if nothing was holding you back?"

Then help that person take one step toward that dream.

8

No Longer Passive

Based on John 9

I listened to the familiar sounds from my usual roadside spot, close enough to gain what little I could from passersby without inviting their anger. The Sabbath was always markedly quieter than other days, without the usual bustle of kids playing and the market humming. Families were together in their homes, resting, worshipping, and eating. I often imagined myself being invited to their table.

Of the few people who noticed me, most considered me a nuisance. I hated it, but I didn't know what else to do. I survived mostly on bread and leftover scraps of food from compassionate passersby. With a full household to clothe and feed, my parents had little to spare for a grown son who should have been helping to support them. I lived embarrassed, aware of my imposition on the world.

A group of men approached. Though I didn't recognize their voices, the question was all too familiar. People seem to assume that broken sight means broken hearing as well. "Rabbi, did the man or his parents sin to cause this blindness?"

It was quiet. Many years ago, I had built defenses against such moments. My skin toughened by the hate and judgment and condemnation. I coexisted with the poisonous words I regularly heard. I'd made my home in them. Something had to be true about what they said. I surely deserved this.

The rabbi knelt down. I could feel His breath and words close. "No one sinned. This happened so that the works of God might be displayed in him."

I was confused. I knew it was the Sabbath, but I heard Him kneading something together, and then His cool hands wiped the mixture on my eyes. He told me to go down to the water and wash my eyes.

I sat with mud on my eyes, torn. The walk down to the water was long, and this was ridiculous. As a child I used to pray to God to heal me, but as an adult such a hope seemed unrealistic and naive.

I had no faith. I had no hope. I'd grown comfortable in my misery, just as I'd numbed myself against the poison of hurtful words.

But this rabbi, He had taken a risk for me. I knew the Law. If anyone saw Him kneading the mixture, they would condemn Him. No one had ever risked something for me before. Few would even speak to me.

I got up, if only out of respect for the man they called Jesus, who defended me and risked His career for me.

Step by cautious step I made my way to the water and washed my eyes. As I lifted my head, color, light, and objects flooded my mind. My senses were overwhelmed by the brilliance and beauty. Even the rusty color of the dirt felt startlingly intense.

I wept. I screamed.

Many people didn't believe me when I returned to my neighborhood and told the tale. They didn't even recognize me despite the decades I'd sat at their feet. Only a few of those who had shown me compassion through the years, they knew it was me.

The Pharisees asked to see me. They demanded to know what had happened, and I told them the truth. I didn't want Jesus to be in trouble, but I did want everyone to know about His power.

The Pharisees summoned Jesus, and for hours I listened as He defended His decision to heal me, a decision condemned by those who cared more about the possibility of a broken rule than the certainty that I had been healed from a life of misery.

I wondered if His ministry was over. Would anyone follow Him now?

The Stream of Risk

One of my heroes in life and in faith is a friend named Kim Patton. I met Kim and her husband, Sherwynn, over six years ago and instantly fell in love because she's a passionate leader and she's a woman who takes risks for the good of others.

Kim and Sherwynn go into prisons and lead something called Restorative Circles, which brings together law enforcement and men and women who have been charged with family violence. Now, Kim is strong and feisty, but she is a little thing. Even so, she sits convicted Black criminals down across from white police officers and walks them through a reconciliation process in which individuals are given the support they need to overcome their life-controlling issues. This process has had a measureable impact on the crime rate in Austin. She believes the racial divide in the justice system can be bridged with relationships and conversations and Jesus. She marches right into the center of some of the deepest, most complicated conflicts in our society. She punches darkness in the face and she makes it look like it's just no big deal.

At my invitation, Kim came to the first IF:Gathering. She knows that I have a heart to see racial unity and diversity happen in our generation. Soon after the event she called me. "Jennie, do you want to go to lunch and talk about how that diversity thing is going at IF?"

A few days later, I showed up at a lunch that I thought would be Kim and me. Instead, four Black women were waiting for me. They all had been at IF:Gathering. It's one thing to sit down to lunch with a table full of Black friends with no agenda, but it's another thing to come to hear how you are doing with diversity in your organization.

I was nervous about what I was about to learn, but I was eager to hear from them. That day over tacos these women began to describe what it feels like to walk into a room of women who look nothing like them and to stare at a stage that represents very few people who look like them. They shared candidly and kindly, and at times it was uncomfortable for them to do so. These women didn't have to come, but not only did they come that day, they leaned in and wanted to stay and help IF mature and grow. After listening, I shared with them my heart for diversity and reconciliation.

Kim, at the end of our meal, said, "I don't think we need to leave this here. I think we need to start our own reconciliation circle."

To which I said, "Like the ones you lead with people who have committed a crime and policemen? You want to lead that with some women from the suburbs?"

"Yep."

"Okay! Let's do it."

A few weeks later we awkwardly set down our hodgepodge of snacks at a local community center. Then we gathered in a circle, several Black women, an Asian woman, a Hispanic woman, and a few white women, not one of us knowing what to expect.

Allison naively talked about being color blind, and then Regina pushed back with the truth of why white people pretending the world is color blind does not help solve problems. She went on to tell the story of her siblings saving money to buy their mother perfume for her birthday. They saved and rode the bus together to the mall (a mall I know well). When they arrived, they were stared at as if they were stealing and they were suspected of shoplifting.

In that moment, every white person in the room stopped talking, stopped assuming. We started to start to change.

We learned to shut up. We learned to listen. Our courageous, gracious new friends of color taught us with great humility and kindness a smidgen of what we didn't understand about the world of privilege. We talked about things that I never knew it was okay to talk about. Each of these women had more to lose than to gain.

Kim fearlessly gathered her friends and risked that we might be insensitive, that we white girls might make things worse. We might not care, we might not come, and we might inflict more hurt on her friends, who had taken a risk in coming.

One of Zac's and my mentors, Rick Taylor, has always taught us that leadership is the willingness to take initiative for the good of others. Kim led for all of our good and for the good of many people we would influence later, though she never could have imagined how God would use us to serve in the future. Instead of apathy and comfort and the easier path, Kim initiated for the benefit of many people and led the way for us to grow and change together.

And because Kim took that risk to initiate, in the coming year we all watched God pull back the curtain to reveal what He is like and give us a fuller picture of what heaven will be. Personally I saw parts of Him and parts of life I didn't even know I was missing. It was the beauty and the creativity and the glorious nature of uniquely crafted individuals, learning to appreciate and love what is different instead of fearing it. I had built a world that looked just like me. In moving outside the box I had erected, I saw more of God. I saw how diverse and good His kingdom is.

Moving into unknowns and uncomfortable places stretches us and gives us more of God.

In various ways we all have been like the Pharisees of Jesus's day, creating a world where we avoid those who aren't like us. Maybe we fear we won't be welcomed by others, so we build boxes with high walls to keep ourselves from getting hurt. Or maybe in our striving to be in the "right" crowd, we build boxes to keep others out. Some of us have defined our box by our life stage or age group or social standing or marital status or denomination or political party. We surround ourselves with people just like us, and the flowing, gorgeous moving ocean full of God's creative awe-invoking diversity becomes a stagnant, unhealthy, gunky pond of goldfish.

Each of us, as we gathered together around that circle, had to set aside any inclination to be defensive or prove to the others that somehow we had all the answers. We had to be willing to face the reality of our own limited perspectives and trust that Jesus was enough to . . .

. . . break down the hurtful walls we had accidentally
　　constructed.

. . . build bridges of sincere friendship and trust as we faced
　　the truth, no matter how difficult.

. . . bond us together despite our differences.

He was enough and then some.

We lived in this world where we were "getting along," but the currents of tension were right under the surface, keeping us from truly experiencing deep friendship with one another. We risked being vulnerable enough to dive into the tensions and awkwardness. We risked exploring the problems we didn't want to admit were even there.

SAFETY IS NOT OUR GOAL

In building relationships with people who are different from us, we have to decide: Are we really willing to risk saying the wrong thing, risk hearing how we are part of the problem? Are we willing to love and push through the hurts that may come?

Why risk our comfort?

Because on the other side of God-oriented, Scripture-informed risk is everything we are looking for: nearness to Jesus; greater faith in His power; deeper, richer experiences and relationships; satisfaction and enjoyment of the short life we have been given.

Our hearts naturally move to self-protection and away from risk-filled leadership and obedience. Although deep in our souls we crave adventure, somewhere on the way toward adulthood or somewhere within it, we stifled that craving with religion, preferring known expectations and controlled, predictable outcomes. We lost our capacity to risk, to explore, to invent, to create, to press into scary new experiences, and we created safe lives where our biggest goal is to measure up and be accepted and be enough.

But Jesus lives on the other side of our comfort zones. The streams we are craving—that He is offering—flow strongest in the spaces we see our need for Him. And as we step out of the boxes we have built, our hearts wake up. The Spirit of God stirs us toward a wild uncontrolled adventure, even if that plays out in the mundane parts of our lives.

I think there should be a God-honoring, obedient risk in our lives every single day. I'm not saying I want that to be true. I'm just saying I believe that Jesus lives on the other side of our comfort. And that when we get comfortable for too long, we start to miss our need for God.

We tend to make most of our decisions based on our fears rather than on our faith. Or we chart our moves based on our pride, believing we are enough in ourselves and we don't need to risk. We don't need to grow, we don't need to help, we don't need anything. We are enough.

These are not modern Western ideas. People believed the same lies in Jesus's day. He continually pressed them out of their comfortable lives, cultural expectations, and predictable scenarios into the risky waters of freedom, healing, fullness, abundance, joy. He pushed them to reconsider everything they believed to be true about themselves and what God values.

It was one thing when Jesus calmed the wild stormy sea one night; but when Jesus called Peter to walk out of the boat on top of that wild sea, He urged him toward a new level of faith. Yes, Peter doubted and started to sink, but Jesus held him up.

Hear me, please. We will never kill our fears, though we tend to spend a lot of time trying to do so; we are called to walk on water—and to do so boldly *despite our fears*. Jesus isn't scolding us for being afraid; He is calling us out of our comfortable boats to do something unthinkable, something that is possible only with His power.

Every time we risk, we place our lives into the hands of our God and test His enoughness. It is for our freedom and joy that we stand out past the limits and confines of our comfort.

What if I told you that to experience God's enoughness you must willingly take risks for the glory of God?

I love that Jesus teaches us about where our abundance will come from before He calls us out on the water. It will not be in our power and striving that anything will happen. Obedient risk will simply be us leaning into His abundance, leaning into His love, simply believing that He will work, believing that He could take any situation and any boring day and cause life change to happen in it.

This isn't just random risk, throwing caution to the wind. This is you stepping out of the boat toward whatever risk God puts in your path, no matter the cost.

This is the way the Spirit moves.

This is the life God calls us toward.

I want to see Jesus in my everyday life, not just when I arrive in heaven. I want to love Him more than I want to appear religious. I want to love people enough to lead them to the One who can heal them. I want to be healed myself. I want to initiate for the good of those around me rather than pad my existence with comfort and ease.

Is there a risk He is calling you toward?

Is there someone outside your circle to befriend? Is there a sin to confess? Is there a person you need to tell about Christ? Is there someone to forgive? Is there a need you are supposed to meet?

There is no safer risk than throwing the weight of your life on an eternal, loving, steadfast God.

THE RISKY BUSINESS OF HEALING

After Jesus healed the blind man on the Sabbath, He was attacked with criticism, doubt, hate, condemnation. He knew it was coming, yet He took the risk. Why? He actually went out of His way to take a risk on this day. He bent down and He kneaded mud with His saliva. This is the step that was clearly against Sabbath ritual.

For our good and for His glory, He risks for us. He risks His reputation. He risks His followers—because everybody is banking on "This is God," and if He sins and in this moment they believe that He sins, they will not follow Him anymore.

And He risks all that for one man's healing.

We each decide whom and how and when we will choose to love. As we go about our days, we often step over the sinners, the broken ones, as if they deserve to be in these positions. Like the religious people that day, we think we need to be the judges when our job is to point the way to healing and participate in the process.

Jesus didn't just heal the blind man on the spot; the beggar had to walk down to the water and wash the mud from his eyes. He risked hope. He risked receiving the love Jesus had shown him, choosing to let down the walls of self-protection he'd erected.

Maybe you have been called to risk big life change, to adopt, to change jobs, or even to move overseas. But we also find ourselves called to risk in the little things, like the risk to rest when tasks and worry call our name. Or the risk to forgive when the wounds go deep. Or the risk to hope when logic says to give up.

The small risks can be trickier. Sometimes making a big, elaborate life change that you know God has called you to is actually easier than forgiving a friend who has hurt you or risking being vulnerable with your small group.

The blind man chose to take the risk. He walked down to that water by himself, and then on the other side of risk, he found healing.

Instead of celebrating, the Pharisees were ticked that Jesus broke the Sabbath. Their vision and compassion were clouded by a determination to prove how great they were. Jesus wasn't having it. He said to them, "For judgment I came into this world, that those who do not see may see, and those who see may become blind."[1]

Jesus highlighted a dichotomy between people who are willing to risk everything to see and people who think they already do see, yet are blind.

The people who think they can see but are actually blind

- think they are capable,
- think they are adequate,
- think they are in control,
- think they don't have need,
- think God has made them "special" and better than others, and
- think they know all the answers to people's problems.

The people who will see because of His healing will

- see their weakness,
- see their inadequacy,
- see God's power,
- see the need around them, and
- see God's infinite ability to meet all their needs.

Jesus was clear: *I came for the sick. Those who are well, those who think they already "see," have no need for a physician.*

Jesus risks for the healing of people, and so should we.

He risked everything and busted through man-made religion and rules to heal a man everyone saw as a burden. Jesus healed a blind man on the Sabbath so that today you are no longer in chains. So that you don't have to wonder for the rest of your life if God sees the brokenness of one individual and will risk everything for your healing.

He wants us to know His ways are for our good. *The Sabbath—do you even know what the Sabbath is for? My plans are for your healing, your restoration.*

Jesus risked everything for our healing, and those of us who have been healed are called to go and give that healing away. We are to risk for others to be healed, risk for others' good, even and especially when we don't feel strong enough or brave enough for the task. We still get out of the boat.

So many individuals are walking away from the church and from God because people have built religious systems they cannot measure up to. They think they are too broken for God because we have acted like they are too broken for us. We have to move from being judges to being healers. God in us is the hope of the world.

ALL FOR THE GLORY OF GOD

One of the most fantastic of God's gifts from our racial bridge-building group was the friendship of a ministry leader in town named Tasha Morrison. Soon after the awkward tacos, she called me on my phone. "Jennie, where are you?"

It was a rare occasion indeed. "I am at the gym."

She said, "Stay there. I am on my way."

I sat just inside at a table, and a few minutes later Tasha walked in with a navy and white Hobby Lobby bag the size of Utah. She hurled it up on the table. I still had not a clue what was about to happen. Tasha sat down, put her hands on top of the bag, and looked directly into my eyes. Now remember this is our second time to meet, and she said, "Jennie, you have a Black son, and you are awfully white. I think God has put me in your life to help you raise your Black son."

Tasha risked possibly offending me because she knew I was open and wanted to learn all I could to be the best mom I can to Coop. She correctly guessed that I'd be more than willing to listen.

Then we started going through the bag together. She had brought me Black hair and skin products I had never heard of, and she walked through how and why we would use each one of them. She brought children's books about Martin Luther King Jr. and others about the gift and complexities of being a kid of color.

Then I pulled out a handful of Black magazines, like *Ebony* and *Essence*. I tilted my head, a bit confused. These obviously were not for Cooper. She said, "Jennie, Coop needs to see leaders of color on your coffee table. He needs to see people who look like him who are successful creators and business leaders. Just put them on your coffee table."

I needed someone to risk my feelings for the greater good, to help me better love my son. Tasha was honest, and I needed to be open to the truth she was sharing, things I would have never understood or considered on my own, in my white world. Tasha probably spent $150 on that enormous bag for my son.

Understanding begins where friendships start. I've found that in my relationship with Tasha. I'm inspired by the risks she's willing to take to cross those racial barriers and help me do the same. Almost every time she comes over, she still puts things in my hand, in my life.

Like this year for the first time, we have a Black Santa for Coop and for our family. Black Santa. We needed Black Santa! Of course I never noticed how white my world was until I got a little color in it. My life was flat missing some of the best parts.

It's amazing what you learn when you build community with those unlike you. I've encountered new words and phrases and ideas I would never have known without these conversations. Stepping outside of sameness expanded my world, and I'm a better person for it.

Tasha shows up for me, and I show up for her. But we both had to be intentional to get to this place. She had to intentionally risk because she believed unity and diversity in our lives was worth it. We had to grant each other permission to be who we are and to say what we think and feel. She gave me the grace and permission to say the wrong things and know she won't run away.

Together we all can risk for the glory of God.

Maybe your risk isn't to start a racial bridge-building group, but some step of risk-filled obedience is waiting for you. What is it?

Recently a friend told me about another woman who was walking through Whole Foods with her two toddlers on her hips (not in a cart, so I'm already thinking, *I don't understand you*). As she shops, she hears a man say, "I don't believe in God."

She keeps walking and God is prompting her, *Go back and talk to him. Go back and pray for him.* And she's got her toddlers. In her arms. At the grocery store.

Let me just tell you in this scenario what Jennie Allen would have done: I'd have thought, *Heck no,* and kept going. I really wouldn't have thought about it again. Except maybe the Holy Spirit is loving enough that He would beat me up and give me a chance to rethink that attitude.

The woman at Whole Foods also keeps going, but she cannot shake the sense she's supposed to talk to the man. So she reluctantly goes back with her two toddlers. She looks at the man, and she says, "Sir, I heard you say that you don't believe in God."

And he says, "Yes, that's right. I don't."

She says, "For some reason, I'm supposed to pray for you. Is that okay? Can I pray for you? I know this is a little weird."

And he says, "Sure. Okay."

In the middle of the grocery store, holding her toddlers, she prays for him. When they look up, he's teary and she asks him, "Why don't you believe in God?"

"Because He's never done anything for me."

She says, "Well, He just made me and my toddlers come across the grocery store to talk to you and pray for you. So you can't use that excuse anymore."

They went on to discuss God and life, and in the middle of the produce section of Whole Foods, his heart was tender toward God.

God wants to move through grocery stores and awkward meals. He wants to move through office happy hours and boot camps. He wants to take what feels like a random thought but is from His Spirit and move into the lives of people around us and, in turn, change ours. **We don't want to miss being part of other people's healing.**

BEYOND OUR IMAGINATIONS

Our racial bridge-building group went on to meet nearly every month, not having any idea what was ahead for our country. The unrest and tension in Ferguson, Missouri, was coming, along with a series of other events that would reveal the racial tension simmering under the surface of the American landscape.

As a naive white person, I don't think I actually believed or thought there was that much racism in the world still. Until our conversations and then Ferguson. How beautiful of God that before Ferguson, before all this upheaval even happened, He put together a tribe of people to do life and ministry together and choose to love each other and do the hard work of risky conversations.

God knew.

And on February 6, 2015, at our second IF:Gathering, several of the women from our circle, led by Tasha Morrison, took the stage with hundreds of thousands of people watching and showed the world torn apart by racial tensions how to have an honest, brave conversation about race and unity.

Thousands of people said they wanted to host "Be the Bridge" to Racial Unity groups in their cities. And today the stories pour in constantly of how God is changing lives.

It all started with Kim initiating an awkward conversation over tacos.

I know you wonder, like I used to, if God is so abundant, why don't we see His abundance everywhere in our lives? These streams that He wants for us, that He longs to pour out of us to a thirsty world, they are always there, flowing right outside of our comfort, right on the other side of the empty wells we keep going to.

Because we were blind and now we see, we can run past the empty jars down to the water and wash the mud off our eyes.

I want to see. I don't want to live blind to God's exquisite story line of healing and beauty happening around me. How do we do that? We step outside the box that represents comfort to us, whatever it is. We step out and watch God start to move beyond our categories, beyond our imagination.

EXPERIENCE GUIDE

BE STILL

Jesus looked at them and said, "With man this is impossible, but with God all things are possible."

Matthew 19:26

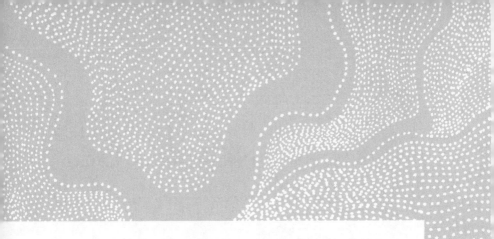

Living with nothing to prove actually makes God-honoring risk a lot more fun. Just as Jesus risked His reputation to set a man free, we are able to more easily see and meet needs around us with less fear when we let go of controlling the circumstances and how our lives appear.

STEP INTO THE STREAM

What is one small or large risk you could take for the glory of God or the good of people?

WADE IN DEEPER

In the next month, visit a church that's new to you or visit a church denomination that is unfamiliar to you. Reflect on what you appreciated about the experience.

QUENCH YOUR THIRST

Do you have diverse friendships? If so, how have they shaped you? What kinds of people intimidate you? What kinds of people do you not pursue? What keeps you from being close?

Hang out with someone different from you this week. Maybe you could meet for tacos!

THE OVERFLOW

Invite people from unique backgrounds to share a meal together. Seek to gather people of different ethnicities, denominations, ages, life stages; and answer these questions together:

1. What do we have in common?

2. How are we unique and what can we learn from each other?

3. How have our differences divided us?

4. What do you need to feel valued and understood?

9

No Longer Afraid

Based on John 11

Something in me knew He wasn't coming. The day was gray, and rain fell gently, as if the sky shared our sorrow. Martha still hoped, staring toward the path that led into our village, but I could see Lazarus fading and all our efforts to make contact with Jesus were exhausted. Surely the news had reached Him. But He hadn't yet come.

He wasn't coming.

Months earlier, sitting at His feet, I was left with one overwhelming and unfamiliar conviction: *Trust.* I wanted to trust Him and keep hoping in this moment, but trust and hope were washing away. Either He knew and chose to withhold His healing, or He was not as powerful as I believed Him to be.

Both possibilities scared me. Our lives had shifted completely to revolve around Jesus. We'd told everyone in our village who we believed Him to be. Most people thought we were crazy, and I could live with that. But what if He wasn't the Messiah? Or what if we just were not important enough to Him?

If Lazarus dies ... Martha and I had no one. We were two single women without a father or mother. How would we provide for ourselves? Who would protect us? Martha and I were strong, but we weren't strong enough for this.

Every local remedy had been exhausted. There was nothing left to do but pray and beg God to save him.

That day my brother died.

Life as we knew it was over. Our beautiful young brother was gone. My grief in losing him was made heavier with anger about our misplaced hope—in a Savior, in heaven, in a good God with a great plan. All that died along with my brother. I felt as if the foundation of my existence was shifting and breaking apart.

The traditional mourning rituals began, and still He didn't come. Each day that He was not here, my doubt grew and the foundation slipped further away.

And then after four days, I heard His voice. Martha ran to Him first, asking why He had not come.

I saw Him coming toward me. There were no words. Only tears. I looked into His eyes, and He was weeping too. His tears dissolved some of my fear. Of course He loved us.

He turned to the tomb and asked that the stone be rolled back. What was He doing? But what could He do now?

He lifted His eyes. "I pray You hear Me. I know You do, but I want my friends here to know that too." I felt as if He had seen straight into my soul, to the doubts that had plagued me for days, and that His prayer was for me. He knew I didn't believe God heard us, that He was good, that He was able. It was as if Jesus could see the wreckage of my faith.

Then He called my brother to come out.

Wrapped in his burial clothes, Lazarus walked out. My dead brother walked into the light. Jesus did not just heal my brother that day; He healed me. My broken faith was restored and my paralyzing fear dissolved by the power of His words. If He could defeat death, there was nothing He could not do.

I will never doubt again. He is here to save the world. And He is powerful enough to do it.

The Stream of Hope

The heart of one of my dearest friends has stopped. In fact, my friend Julie Manning even has Lazarus beat. She has brushed death three times. Various heart conditions have led to her being resuscitated several times.

Julie does a lot of life beside me, and one day after we'd studied this story of Lazarus together with hundreds of other women in Austin, we sat in my car in the parking lot and I had the privilege of discussing death with someone who daily lives so near to it. As we processed the evening and what we had studied, she said, "Jennie, have you ever wondered if Jesus cried that day because He was about to pull Lazarus away from heaven?"

I stared at my friend who has faced death many times and whose broken heart could take her to heaven at any moment, realizing she contains the same backward vision as Jesus. At the core of my friend isn't a fear of death; it is an ache for heaven.

If we could actually believe that on the other side of this life are the best parts, then what would we have left to fear? If we could believe that we have nothing to fear even in death, I'm convinced we could get on with living. There would still be trials. There would still be suffering. There may even be darkness that makes us wish for death. However, if we could quit being so afraid of dying, we could start to live.

But as long as we grasp for our lives, trying to control them, we are losing them. We all have dreams for our lives, for our kids, for our careers, for our ministries, for our friendships. We have expectations of how our lives will turn out. When our hopes are in those dreams for our lives—spoiler alert!—they are always disappointed. Because even if many of your dreams come true, they'll never fill your soul like you thought they would.

We try to avoid suffering—suffering that we need to face. Romans 5 directs us to lean into suffering so that we learn to persevere, so that we are filled with hope, so that we find joy.[1] Which is why many of the people you know who have suffered most are also most full of joy. A backward way of life: that is what Jesus calls us to. This life is not enough to fill us, but Jesus is so completely sufficient that it doesn't matter.

Julie's house has flooded four times in the past year from different causes. I'm not kidding and I'm not exaggerating. It's as if she's under attack by a flood demon. The worst flood came from a busted pipe. It ruined all of their downstairs, all of their furniture. She and John and the kids had to move out of their house and into a tiny apartment while their home was reconstructed.

Of course as her friends, we were all worried, but she just kept saying in the sweetest little voice you ever did hear, "It's okay."

We said, "Julie! You just moved out of your house and all your possessions are wet and only half of it is covered by your insurance."

She continued smiling and said with certainty and sincerity, "Jennie, I promise this is all going to be okay."

Something about daily living with the reality that she may go home to be with Jesus, something about tasting death, something about her nearness to Jesus and her hope in her forever home, has shifted her perspective. Holding this life loosely changes everything here.

Dreams here can be shattered or our best dreams can be realized, yet compared to the surpassing glory of knowing Christ, we can consider everything a loss. As the apostle Paul says, in essence, I consider the dreams here, both those disappointed and those achieved, garbage, that I may gain Christ and be found in Him.[2]

But do we really share that attitude? I'm not sure I do, much of the time. See, I don't trust God the way Julie does. Do you? Because I think that if we did, we would be more free. Why? Because we would know that we are already free. Nothing in this world has a hold on us.

Those of us who have Jesus and are found in Him . . .

- We are free of worry about this life working out perfectly, because a perfect eternal life is coming.
- We are free of guilt and shame, because we have been completely forgiven.
- We are free of all fear, because who or what on this earth would we fear if God is with us?
- We get to stop being afraid. Fear has no power over people who aren't afraid of the very worst being thrown at them.

A while back, Julie and I met for lunch, back when my backpack was still securely strapped on. I was growing disillusioned. Everywhere I looked, those I love were suffering. Doubt and fear had crept in.

Where was Jesus in this darkness? Was He not strong enough to protect us? Was He not good?

"Julie, you are one hundred percent sure that there is life after death, that Jesus is real?"

She looked at me like I was a crazy fool. "Yes, Jennie. One hundred percent sure."

Her heart is weak, and God could just take her home any day, any second. So she says, "One hundred percent sure," and it means something to me.

When not even death scares you, there isn't much to be worried about. Floods, toddlers, money issues, home loss . . . no big deal. Julie is unshaken by the worst the enemy throws because he cannot steal the hope and future that means the most to her. Her faith builds mine.

What We Find Inside Suffering

I wonder, is it possible that you are reading this and your whole world or a piece of it is falling apart? This is where I want to grab two chairs and some coffee. And I would grab your shoulders and hug you and cry with you and pray with you. This is where I would listen instead of talk.

That long awkward space is me listening.

I am just so sorry. I hate suffering. I hate the brokenness of this world. I hate that one of my best friends had a massive stroke and still can't talk. I hate that my son has eight-year-old friends in Rwanda who are living on the streets. I hate the cancer several of my friends are fighting. I hate that children are abused. I hate death. I hate it! All of it!

So does God.

We live in a fallen, broken world. The goal is not that we make sense of suffering, because we can't. The goal is that we wouldn't fear suffering.

In the story of Lazarus, we read that Jesus allows some of the people He loves most on earth to face death. For four long days they wait in the darkness. Wondering if He is coming. Wondering if He loves them. Wondering if He is powerful.

Why does He do it? He says, "For your sake I am glad that I was not there, so that you may believe."[3]

Faith is built through suffering, but only when we lean into it and lean into Him. "The heavens declare the glory of God."[4] And I believe that suffering makes us long for that glory in ways that we never would if everything worked out perfectly always.

Jesus has a plan for our suffering, but it is so difficult to see it in the long, dark wait.

Jesus led His people, whom He so dearly loved, to the darkest place, a grave, to shine the brightest truth to produce the most glorious hope and faith.

Goodness, that is difficult to believe, though. Sometimes when I go there, when I go to the darkest parts of my story or the stories around me, when I glimpse the pain and suffering that our loving God doesn't spare us from, I feel desperately afraid.

I am afraid He isn't good enough.

I am afraid He isn't powerful enough.

I am afraid He doesn't love us enough.

And guess what happens next? I go numb. I pick numb over fear. I pick numb over despair. I pick numb over moving into my own pain or anyone else's.

We often go numb because we think we can't handle the darkness: the darkness in us, the darkness around us. Our hearts grow tired of carrying hurt, and it feels much easier to disengage. The lie we believe is that a full life is a life without pain. But as we move through the dark, we search frantically for God, not for ideas about Him but for God Himself. He is there, right past our idea of a perfect comfortable life.

Emotions are designed by God to point to an ache for Him and for heaven. Emotions are compasses, not destinations. We don't ignore them and we don't camp out in them, but we let them show us the places God wants to meet us and the places we need to do work.

Jesus has a plan for our suffering, but that cannot be accomplished if we keep trying to push it into a safe, tidy place in our closet. His plans in us are accomplished as we move into the pain. We can face the suffering because Jesus is there in the midst of it.

Right now, you may be thinking, *How does this change my every day? Nobody is dying today. I am just not measuring up as a friend, as a coworker, as a mother, as a leader.*

Well, the Jesus who can overcome our physical death is the same One who will overcome the little everyday deaths and set us free from our fears. The gospel is the story of dead people coming alive. But we cannot raise ourselves. In ourselves we are not enough to even modify our behavior. We don't seem to have the power to go from disappointment, fear, sadness, and bondage to lives of freedom, joy, and love.

We need radical soul revival.

If anything on earth exposes our not-enoughness, it is death. Can dead people pull themselves up and out of a pit? Nope, they are dead. Death is the absence of power. Death is the absence of ability. Death is the absence of life. Ephesians 2 starts by saying we were all dead in our sin. Dead. No hope. No way out. Dead.

This declaration is followed by two words that change everything: "But God."

We have no power over death . . . *but God.*

We have no power over our sin . . . *but God.*

We have no power to change . . . *but God.*

"But God, being rich in mercy . . . made us alive together with Christ" even when we were dead.[5]

I am certain you did not pick up this book because you were worried about missing the *very worst* parts of your life: the suffering, the pain, the trials, the conflict, the darkness.

But what if, in trying to miss the worst parts of life, we are also missing the best?

WITH EVERYTHING AND WITH NOTHING?

My sister, Katie, is incredibly creative. She is a designer in Arkansas, and the girl just can't help it—she makes beauty without even trying that hard. It's her gift.

Not long ago we sat in her kitchen, one of the loveliest I have ever seen, enjoying pizza while our kids played outside on her Slip'N Slide. Months earlier she had found a fixer-upper, and, well, she had fixed it up! The house was so darling and homey and perfect. It almost hurt to walk through it because you just love it so much.

Now my sister is gifted, but my sister is also deep. She loves Jesus, and she desperately wants to see her life poured out for Him. That day she wondered aloud something I have thought at least a thousand times. "Jennie, I have a cute house. I have great kids. My life is really happy right now—and I feel guilty. Is it okay to be happy?"

I was struck by my sister's question. The answer didn't feel completely obvious to me.

My sister's happy darling world came crumbling down a few months ago. As I sat next to her on a curb outside a restaurant, a five-minute phone call—*poof*—changed her life forever.

Every day since then, if we aren't together, we talk on the phone, sometimes five times a day. Often I have called her and she is reading her Bible if she isn't with her children. I always say, "Oh no, I don't want to interrupt you reading your Bible." And she says, "It's okay. I'm always reading my Bible." When we were all together over Christmas, every time I couldn't find her, she would be in her room with her Bible and journal.

She told me, "Jennie, His Word has become my hope. Heaven has become my home. These words have become the way that I get up in the morning and the way that I grieve and the way that I take care of my kids."

On a rainy day, we drove together to her cute new house to help her pack up her stuff before she put her house on the market. Through no fault of her own, she was staring at a life without her job, without her community, without her friends, without her church, without her husband. I have never felt more like a protective big sister. I've been so overwhelmingly worried about her.

That day as I drove, she stared out the window not talking much. Seemingly out of the blue she turned toward me and said something that is still changing me. "Jennie, how blessed am I to lose everything all at once? To know that with nothing else on earth, God is enough? For the rest of my life, I will know I only need Him and that He really is that good."

My sister reminds me of the apostle Paul: "I know what it is to be in need, and I know what it is to have plenty. I have learned the secret of being content in any and every situation, whether well fed or hungry, whether living in plenty or in want."[6]

What was his secret? What is her secret?

I can do all this through and with our Jesus who gives me strength.[7] In other words, when we do not have enough or feel enough, we believe Jesus is enough. It is the mercy of God to allow all of our dreams here to come true and find that they all disappoint and nothing on earth but Him will ever satisfy us. It is also the mercy of God to let us lose everything on earth and see even then that He is enough for us.

Following Jesus does result in our happiness; it is just a backward way to it. Happiness, fearlessness, and freedom are found by moving toward the things that we most often tend to avoid.

I love how Jesus spells it out for us in the beatitudes in Matthew 5, where every line begins with the Greek word *makarios*. That word is often translated into English as "happy."

So Jesus says, here's who the happy people will be:

Happy are the poor in spirit, for theirs is the kingdom of heaven.

Happy are those who mourn, for they shall be comforted.

Happy are the meek, for they shall inherit the earth.

Happy are those who hunger and thirst for righteousness, for they shall be satisfied.

Happy are the merciful, for they shall receive mercy.

Happy are the pure in heart, for they shall see God.

Happy are the peacemakers, for they shall be called sons of God.

Happy are those who are persecuted for righteousness' sake, for theirs is the kingdom of heaven.

Maybe you are thinking, *Then I don't think I want to be one of the happy people.* I get it. I have the same response.

But in reality, there's no escaping it: every one of us will face difficulty, pressure, grief, pain. Where will we turn in those moments?

The happy people are the free people.

The happy people are the ones who aren't addicted to this world, whose hope is in heaven.

The happy people are the ones who don't fear losing anything on earth because their hope isn't here.

The happy people are the ones who taste suffering and know that Jesus is enough.

The happy people are the ones who need God and have God!

Oswald Chambers wrote, "God's aim looks like missing the mark because we are too short-sighted to see what He is aiming at."[8]

God is aiming for our freedom and our salvation, but what it takes to get that, we barely understand.

When my sister is walking through the deep dark waters, I look at her standing on her tippy-toes in the deep, gasping for air, and I want to punch something. I want a boat to whisk her away and bypass the suffering. But that is not what she would say. She would say this is where she sees God issue breath. This is where she knows He is real.

Most of us fear suffering, but as I watch some who are so dear to me walk through the dark times, I say you and I should fear if we never suffer, fear if we never need God.

I am so comforted that Jesus wasn't looking at Mary and Martha to prove their faith to Him; He actually was there to prove His power to them.

You may be suffering more than I can possibly imagine right now. I'm just so sorry.

I won't offer trite answers. I won't give you something to stick on your heart that says, "You should feel better and believe God because _____." I won't do that.

But I do believe Jesus pours His streams of hope into our suffering, and I believe we'll find abundance and life there. I believe that.

I'm fighting to believe that.

I'm fighting to believe that when hell pours down on someone I love here, heaven in some way is being built. I've seen it happen. Sarah Henry, my dear friend who has been recovering from a massive stroke for the past three years, tears up every time I tell her about the many people who have told me that they have trusted Christ because of watching her life. Her stroke took her words but not her joy. Even without her voice, she has shared Jesus with more people than most of us. But even seeing that, I can't understand how all the difficulty is working out for good. I continue to say to Him, *I don't get it—but where am I going to go but You?*

I am sticking with the only One I know who has beat death. I've found that He pushes us into the suffering and into the pain because, in those deaths, both large and small, He knows we will turn to Him for courage, for the hope that something is happening beyond what we can see right here, right now.

He is real and the stories that He writes are good. Yes, they have dark chapters, but all good stories need dark chapters so the light can shine through.

He is enough, so we can live fearless—unshaken by darkness or death or danger.

Our God is working toward a world where there is no more suffering, and that is where you and I are headed. That is the story line we are living. He hates death. He hates sin. He hates pain. He is about destroying it. But in the meantime, He is redeeming it for epic purposes, and one day we'll know His purposes were worth it.

Knowing that you may be suffering today or feeling fearful about the future, I just can't write a little ending here and move on until I pray for you, for all of us.

God, it is for Your glory that we exist, and we are created for You. You just picked up some dirt and made us. And I don't understand it, but I know that You are able to do anything. We are so finite, we are so limited, and yet our lives feel long. And our time here feels eternal; especially, God, when we are suffering, it feels like it's never going to end. We have no perspective; we have no hope. And then You say things that are crazy, like, "It is better that I go away because I'm preparing a place for you."[9]

But, Jesus, as I read the story of You and Your people here, I just picture You gradually leading us all into deeper depths and to a dark grave. And then You walk in, and You conquer that. Your light shines in the very darkest places. So because of that, I'm praying that You would help my friend reading these words to believe that You are enough for the darkest places in her life.

God, help us not pretend that life is easy and great and fine. Help us admit what is hard and celebrate what is great. And help us come home to You ready, ready for all to be right and well again. Amen.

EXPERIENCE GUIDE

BE STILL

Even though I walk through the valley
of the shadow of death,
I will fear no evil,
for you are with me;
your rod and your staff,
they comfort me.

Psalm 23:4

Lately it seems as if every day brings news of another terrorist attack in the world. The goal of terrorism isn't that it would destroy the world; it's that the world would live afraid. And, my friend, our fear is something we can control.

Romans 8 says,

> Who shall separate us from the love of Christ? Shall tribulation, or distress, or persecution, or famine, or nakedness, or danger, or sword? . . . No, in all these things we are more than conquerors through him who loved us. For I am sure that neither death nor life, nor angels nor rulers, nor things present nor things to come, nor powers, nor height nor depth, nor anything else in all creation, will be able to separate us from the love of God in Christ Jesus our Lord.[10]

The most precious, life-giving thing about us—our identity in Christ—can never be taken from us.

STEP INTO THE STREAM

Write down brief answers to the following questions:

- What is the worst thing that could happen?

- So what happens if that comes true?

- So what happens because of that?

- So what happens because of that?

When you reach the end of the "so what happens," there lies your greatest fear, the one that keeps you in bondage. When you can name that, consider this:

- Would God be enough for your greatest fear?

WADE IN DEEPER

Write down in your own words Psalm 23 as a personal note from God to you.

QUENCH YOUR THIRST

Share your big fear with your small group or a close friend. Discuss together what it would look like to live unafraid of it. Have each person share her fear.

Head to a nearby pond or lake. Write the fear on a rock and throw it in. And *leave it there for good*. What truth about God makes this possible?

THE OVERFLOW

Look for people who are suffering and find a way to encourage them. Grab some friends and visit a local homeless shelter, prison, nursing home, or hospital. You don't even have to bring anything; just go talk to people. Look them in the eyes and hear their stories. Be with them. Practice the ministry of presence.

No Longer Ashamed

Based on John 13

We'd taken our seats quickly. The tension felt thick. The room buzzed with the slow murmur of voices, everyone concerned about the escalating anger toward Jesus we'd felt on the street.

I saw Jesus stand up and take off His outer garments. *What is He doing?*

He slowly wrapped a towel around His waist and picked up the basin of water near the door. My heart dropped. I knew. I looked down at my feet, caked thick with dirt. Where were the servants who usually did this chore? I'd noticed when we sat down that no one had washed our feet, but I didn't even consider doing it. And now Jesus was taking up the task?

Bent low over Matthew's feet, our teacher, the Son of God, looked more like a servant.

I couldn't stand it. The Son of God reduced to washing our dirty feet.

When He came to me, I quickly pulled back my foot. "No. You cannot do this, Jesus."

He reached out again for my foot. "If I do not do this, Peter, you have no part of Me. This is the entrance to My new way. We begin here, Peter. All that I am about to reveal to you begins here."

I wanted Him, I wanted His way, I wanted in. "Then wash all of me!"

But it was my feet He had to wash, the dirtiest part of me. And I would have to let Him.

"Put out your dirty foot, Peter."

I felt ashamed. I regretted not getting up earlier when I noticed that the servants hadn't come to wash our feet. I felt embarrassed my feet were so dirty. I felt uncomfortable as the others at the table sat in silence, watching our leader wash my feet. I felt terrifyingly vulnerable.

He said, "Unless I wash your feet, you have no part in Me."

He was offering something I hadn't even known I needed. But He knew. He knew what was coming even that night. The very feet He was washing would carry me lying and running from Him. If I could go back to that night I would say, "Wash my feet, Jesus. Scrub harder. Clean me and tell me I am right with You, I am part of You.

"And when I start to run, hold me to You."

I didn't say those words to Him that night, but that is what He did. That is what He does.

The Stream of Grace

I sat between my two girls in the most humble of church services with dark ash on our foreheads. It bothered me to see their foreheads smudged with dark ash. I wanted to defend them. They are pretty pure-hearted almost always. My youngest one still twiggy and naive to most of the darkness in the world. My older one cries easily when she learns of people suffering, whether across the cafeteria or around the world. I wanted them to be above the dark soot representing our human, fallen, dark hearts, all prone to wander and sin.

Ashes to ashes. Dust to dust.

No human is separate from this reality.

We are all so terribly small and fragile. The ash reminds us of it. We hate to be reminded of it.

The ash felt heavy on my forehead too. But unlike my optimism concerning my darling girls, I knew it belonged there.

The ash. It screams that I don't measure up, that I am small, I am broken, I am a sinner, and I am dust. It feels heavy but it feels right. The ash is the right message to the world. It is my physical proclamation. *I know!* I know I am not enough. I know I need God. I know I sin.

In the weeks and months leading up to that moment, most of the people looking on would judge my life and think I was pretty good, or at least that I was trying to be.

But I knew. I'd felt distant from God, and that usually is because of sin. I knew that . . .

I often live driven more than I live called.

I've wanted to not fail more than I've wanted to see God save souls.

I've wanted a God I could predict and control more than I've wanted a rush of His uncontrollable Spirit.

I've tried to prove myself at the expense of loving well.

I've wanted to be seen more than to see.

I've doubted God more than believed Him.

Yes, all of that. I need God and my girls do too, and we always will.

We don't confess so that God will forgive; we confess to remember and enjoy that we already are forgiven. Jesus has handled this problem fully and completely and replaced our sin with His goodness.

But our enemy is after us, and he wants us to believe the lie that this dirt defines us, that we are frauds for speaking of Jesus when we have sin in us. He wants us to doubt our freedom and doubt our God.

So let's call his bluff and say what is true.

Yep. I sin. I am a sinner.

So many of our problems come when imperfect people try to act as if they have it all together. We all have been there. And what's the result? We hide behind images we create of happy, clean, impressive lives. We are exhausted. Because if you create an image to hide behind, you'll have to spend all your energy holding it up.

When the goal becomes being liked, no amount of approval ever feels like enough.

When the goal becomes a bigger platform, no platform ever feels big enough.

When the goal becomes more money, no amount of money ever feels like enough.

When the goal becomes success, no promotion or award or sales numbers will quite cut it.

And when the goal becomes being thin or beautiful, no number on a scale ever feels like you've finally arrived.

In the years that I fought my eating disorder, I hated it. I wanted to stop caring about my weight and appearance. I remember wondering how I could ever retrain my brain to stop focusing so much on myself.

For many, their eating disorders progress to the stage where medical intervention is needed. But in my case the bottom line was that my thought life was just completely consumed with food and what to eat or not eat and when to work out. My brain hovered there as if it were stuck on a TV channel, with no remote and no way to turn it off or switch to a different program.

It had never occurred to me that this was sin that needed to be confessed and that God had given me the power to "take every thought captive to obey Christ."[1]

I remember the day those words leaped off the pages of my thick dark-green study Bible, soon after I learned I was pregnant for the first time. I reread and reread them. In shock as I realized that my thoughts were mine to control. It was the first time I got on my knees and confessed my addiction to my image and my worship of control. I asked God to help me take my thoughts captive. The concept thrilled me. Maybe it was possible to escape this prison of self-hate and control, and with the knowledge of a new life growing in me, I had even more motivation to make a shift in my thinking.

Healing rarely happens overnight. But now I wasn't alone in the fight. When thoughts flooded my mind about what I could or couldn't eat or when and how I would exercise or weigh again, when I would pass a mirror or zip up my pants or look at a menu, or when someone noticed or talked about my weight, through every anxiety that invaded, I clung to Jesus. I thought of Him, I talked to Him, I asked for His help, I asked for His perspective, I read His Word, I recited verses that came to mind. So now flooding my brain alongside the obsessive thoughts was Jesus and His love for me and His words.

And over time the truth of Jesus changed my perspective. He freed me, thought by thought, hour by hour, day by day. And while I couldn't say exactly when it happened, one day I woke up and I knew I was free.

I spent a lot of my life trying to be perfect. And that's an exhausting way to live.

The fact is, I'm not perfect. And now I choose regularly to display my imperfections. I don't get to be as awesome as my ego would like to be, but I get to enjoy the places God has me rather than fight to keep myself somewhere I never deserved to be. I get to be free to be known by God and those closest to me.

I pick that. **I pick being the sinner and letting God get the glory.**

Nobody wants your fake perfect version. Nobody. Not God, not your people, and not you.

THE END OF PRETENDING

Every once in a while I get around someone whose soul is full of God. Their souls are so content, Jesus is just coming out of them. Do you know people like that? It is so refreshing. It is beautiful. They are not needy. They're not trying to prove themselves. They're not trying to measure up. They're not trying to get your attention or affection. They hold no judgment for others because they are aware of their own sin.

My grandmother lived this way. We called her Gaga, though as we got older she insisted on Grandmother. An elegant lady raised in the Deep South, she loved Jesus, though faith was private for her and she rarely wore her spirituality for others to see. Rather than talk about Jesus, she lived like Jesus. She was at home in her skin, and she put others at ease as well.

She was self-deprecating and deeply aware of her own shortcomings. As her grandkids, we did so many things over the years that should have disappointed her. She should have judged us and told us how out of line we were. But she always left the judging to God and pulled us in all the closer.

She knew grace and she gave it away. It all was rooted in her understanding of the amazing grace that saved a wretch like her. Faith and the gospel were simple and real to her. She didn't need to wax eloquent over theological points; she just chose to love, to never speak ill, to believe the best, and to let God be God. No need to try to be a god when He was plenty good at His job.

Something about her core identity was altogether different from most of the world's. She wasn't trying to impress anyone. She also wasn't defined by and in bondage to her sin. She was forgiven and free, and her life gave that away.

Grace breathes more grace.

Who are you?

Are you impressive?

Or are you broken?

Or are you forgiven?

In John 13 we look on as God, who owns every universe, pours water in a basin and begins to wash the disciples' feet, to wipe them with a towel that was wrapped around Him. His identity drove His humility. Jesus was the Son of the almighty God; He was clear and secure in that fact. Therefore He had nothing He was grasping for. He had nothing to prove here or to these men.

When you have nothing to protect and nothing to prove, God moves through you.

When you have nothing to protect and nothing to prove, you know freedom.

Of course He comes to Peter, and Peter does what all of us would have wanted to do. *Lord, no. You can't wash my feet.* And he pulls back his dirty foot.

We do not want to put our dirt out. We are on pedestals. We are in positions that seem to require our perfection and our morality. Yet when we pull our dirt back, we miss our need for God and we miss any real depth with other people.

When Zac and I planted the church in Austin, we didn't want a place where people would come and feel a need to pretend they were okay and that they had it together. We told our small band of a launch team that we believed every one of us was a recovering sinner and needed to treat that seriously. Zac called our whole church to a twelve-step program called Celebrate Recovery. It is a tool developed for churches, similar to an AA program for addicts.

Everyone was shocked, unsure their sin was bad enough to need such a big commitment. Yet, slowly, some of the most godly, seemingly perfect people began to enter small groups and go through the process of coming face to face with their sin and tendency to seek hope in things of this world.

In those months our small band of leaders confessed, some for the very first time in their lives,

- decades of unforgiveness,
- pornography addictions,
- abortions,
- sexual sin,
- alcohol dependencies,
- addictions to approval, and
- overwhelming debt they had been hiding.

A few months into this, after our initial launch of about five groups, our core team members looked at one another and said, "If these issues are hiding in our small church, imagine how many people are hiding their issues and struggles around the world."

It terrified me that we have accidentally built an institution in direct opposition to the call of Christ for the church. We should be the safest place on earth to bring our sin. We are the only ones that can offer hope for it!

The power of the Holy Spirit swept forward in the coming years through that surrendered, brave, free, forgiven group of people in ways I had never seen before. Instead of all our fears coming true—that we would be rejected, that we would be judged, that we would be shamed—the exact opposite happened.

People were set free. People experienced the grace and forgiveness of Christ like never before. People grew closer and more connected than they had ever been before. Healing and restoration became contagious, and people who got close to us didn't even want to hide.

Our church rallied around each person and met needs. When someone confessed debt he had been hiding, the small group rallied to help pay it off and to hold that person accountable to not fall back in. When someone confessed pornography addictions, the small group rallied to help build protection and accountability in that person's life. It was a wildfire of holiness, and it wasn't legalistic. It was the most life-giving, community-building, God-honoring revival I have ever seen.

We don't just confess our sin; we throw in with each other, point each other to the One who forgives and gives us the power to fight it! We have grown apathetic about sin, my friend. We have let it take hold in our lives, and in the dark it has all the power.

"Therefore confess your sins to each other and pray for each other so that you may be healed."[2]

Exposing Our Dirt

We are ashamed of the dirt of our lives, but Jesus wants to move right into it. Jesus goes to the very dirtiest part of the disciples and invites them to need Him.

I have often heard Jesus washing the disciples' feet taught as the example of servant leadership, that this is how we should lead others. And sure, later Jesus mentions that we are to serve others as He served them. It's a good lesson. It is a correct interpretation of the passage.

However, it isn't His main point at this moment.

This moment, by the way, is terrifying to Peter because he is thinking, *I respect You, Jesus. I worship You. I follow You. I do not want You washing my feet. I don't want You stooped down cleaning the worst parts of me.* Peter still wanted to prove himself on his own, without God.

But Jesus said, *This is not a small thing, Peter. This is not about you eating here with clean feet. This is about your soul being clean.*

Jesus's men had all been trying to measure up, trying to be the greatest, trying to hide their dirt, still thinking that God wanted their performance, when all He wanted was their souls. Just as He wants ours.

Peter's faith was real and his salvation secure, yet Jesus was clear: he still must have his feet washed. Each of us needs a regular cleansing of our souls that leads to freedom. But we often separate ourselves from other people, and we tuck away our sin because we don't know what to do with it. We don't want to put out our dirt.

And I think that Jesus is saying to us, *Hey, if you believe Me, if you believe that I can wash your foot, if you believe that I can wash your soul, why would you not put it out there?* A dirty foot only needs one thing: to be washed clean. Ultimately, that is what Peter and all of us need.

All our inclinations to strive and prove ourselves point to our need to be rescued. **Our greatest needs begin to be filled when we admit we have great needs and turn to the only One able to meet them.**

"If we say we have no sin, we deceive ourselves, and the truth is not in us. If we confess our sins, he is faithful and just to forgive us our sins and to cleanse us from all unrighteousness."[3] It's terrifying to put it out there and admit our need, just as Peter experienced. Right now, you are thinking about closing this book and pretending you never read it. But you want to be on the other side of this, I promise. You want to be clean and free.

A word that I rarely hear anymore is *repentance.* The word *repent* means "to turn away."

The Christian life can be summed up in three words: *repent and believe.* You confess all your sin, the worst of it, and you believe the truth of God.

We agree with God about our sin, and we don't just confess it, but we let the cleansing stream of Jesus's grace pull us away from our sin. This will take humility. In my experience, humility usually involves a bit of humiliation. Every time I am honest about my struggles and honest about my sin and honest about my pride and honest about the mistakes I've made and honest about the sin in my soul, I find it humiliating.

And do you know what happens right after I confess it?

I immediately feel kind of small. I immediately feel all the things that I don't want to feel—the shame, the fear, the isolation, the embarrassment. I do feel them for a minute. I feel caught.

I let that feeling wash over me because the next wave coming is relief. I actually get to be cleansed now, and the shame that I've been feeling, that inevitably had affected me and everyone around me, starts falling off and recedes with the waves of grace. I find grace and I find connection to Jesus again, a deep, honest, sincere-in-my-soul kind of connection with God, because I've admitted I need Him and I'm close to Him again and we're right.

Maybe you have been doing things for God for a long time, but you've never really had this kind of relationship with Him. Maybe you are thinking, *I don't know if the Spirit of God is in me. I don't know if I've ever trusted Jesus Christ as Lord and Savior.*

Do you go to Jesus with your sin regularly?

Do you experience His forgiveness?

Enjoying His grace does cost us something. One thing: death. Death of our old selves. Death of our pride. Death of thinking we can be enough on our own. It's hard; it's messy. You will hate it for a moment. But you know what happens in your soul? You get free. You know what happens when you are free? Other people are set free. When you put your dirt out first, everybody else gets to do the same. It's contagious. Other people are freed through our honesty and confession. We don't need to tell the world; we just need to tell a few warrior friends who won't settle for our being plastic or fake.

We expose our dirt because Jesus has the power to wash it and free us from bondage to it. **God's grace is exquisite and enough for the dirt that seems impossible to clean.**

We want to see revival happen in our places. We want to see God move in the souls of people while we are alive, however long that is. Yes? We want that.

It starts with us. If we are not moved by the Spirit of God, why on earth would anyone else ever be moved? If we don't experience His forgiveness and His grace on a regular basis, then how could we give away His forgiveness and grace to anybody else?

THE GREAT EXCHANGE

Jesus knew that in a few hours Peter was going to deny Him and that for the next three days Peter was going to feel distant from Him and that he was going to feel rejected by Him.

Peter loved so passionately, and he made some of the biggest mistakes. He was prideful and passionate. We are just like Peter.

We are zealots.

We are sinners.

Jesus knows this.

And Jesus knows what Peter doesn't know yet. *You do need this. You do need My forgiveness. You don't even know what you are capable of. But you need this forgiveness today.*

I wash your pride that thinks that I need you.

I wash your doubt that you think I can't handle.

I wash your fear that stops you from obeying.

I wash your shame that makes you hide.

I wash your independence that makes you think you don't need Me.

I wash your performance that you think proves your worth.

I wash your betrayal that haunts you.

I wash your arrogance that resists your need of forgiveness.

I wash your striving for your own name.

I wash your love for your own honor.

I wash your mistakes that you cannot name.

I wash your anger that lashes out sometimes.

I wash your feet and set them on My path—a path of service, a path of love, a path of rejection, a path of suffering, a path of joy, a path of setting people free.

A few hours after He washed the feet of Peter, Jesus chose to die on the cross to wash all our filth and dirt away. In one violent, costly act, He washed us of all our sin. We were needy, and Christ became sin and paid the penalty of that sin so that we would be with Him forever. His blood in exchange for ours.

Repent and believe. This is what it looks like to fill our souls with streams of living water, bread that does not ever leave us hungry again, and light that takes over the darkness. **We are not defined by our worst or our best; we are defined by our God.**

We put out our dirt and we let Jesus wash it and then we go tell everybody about it.

Is your heart hard? Does God feel distant?

This is the road back. Repent and believe.

EXPERIENCE GUIDE

BE STILL

If we say we have fellowship with him
while we walk in darkness, we lie and
do not practice the truth. But if we
walk in the light, as he is in the light,
we have fellowship with one another,
and the blood of Jesus his Son cleanses
us from all sin. If we say we have no sin,
we deceive ourselves, and the truth is
not in us.

1 John 1:6–8

The first time I remember hearing a public confession, my little perfection-seeking self stood jaw-dropped, stunned. I was watching a man share his most shameful dark secret in front of hundreds of people. Hearing his broken repentance undid me. And it made me wonder, *What if instead of hiding my sin I'm supposed to bring it out in the open?*

Guess what? We are. We have nothing to prove to anyone, to ourselves, or to God, because Christ has proved it for us.

STEP INTO
THE STREAM

What sin are you afraid to bring to Jesus?

WADE IN DEEPER

Write a letter from God to you concerning your sin. What would God say to you about His love and forgiveness for you?

QUENCH
YOUR THIRST

Identify patterns in your life that keep you from confessing your sin. Get a few note-cards and write out some verses that remind you of the truth of God's grace when you fall into one of those patterns of shame. Stick those verses everywhere—in your car, on your bathroom mirror, on your bedside table.

THE OVERFLOW

Go on a walk with a mentor or friend you trust and share what God is teaching you about His grace. Ask each other these questions:

1. Where are you craving grace?

2. In the past, how have you experienced God's grace in your life?

3. What is keeping you from bringing your sin to Jesus?

No Longer Empty

Based on John 21

Jesus had appeared to us, so we knew He was alive. But we were lost. What did He want us to do?

I was certain there was nothing left for me with Him. Judas had betrayed Him. I had betrayed Him. The guilt of my sin and betrayal that had tormented me in His death was raging worse now that He had returned. I would eventually be face to face with Him. What could I say or do to prove my regret, to prove my love?

I grabbed the most familiar thing to me, my nets, and several other men followed me to the boat. Something about being on the water always calmed me. But this time the waters only reminded me of Him. It would be easier if He wasn't who He said He was. But I'd walked on the water, I'd seen the wine made out of water, I'd held the overflowing baskets of bread and fish, I'd hugged Lazarus after he was brought back to life.

I'd seen enough to know Jesus was God. And I had failed Him.

It was late when Thomas and James helped me throw out our net. It was strangely quiet on the water. No fish. Even the pursuits I used to be good at were telling me what I knew already. *I am a failure. I know. I don't need more empty nets to tell me so.*

I sat down in the boat. My soul ached. I was no longer at home anywhere.

Just as the sun peeked out, a man on the shore yelled to us, "Do you have any fish?"

I was uninterested. James shouted back, "None!"

"Try the other side of the boat," the man replied. "You will find some."

What a fool, I thought to myself. There were no fish; we'd been out all night. How could He possibly know more from shore than we knew on the water? But a few of the men did as He said. The boat started to rock. The force of fish swimming into the net nearly capsized us.

What was happening?

I stood up and looked out toward the man on shore. And I knew. It was Jesus.

Without thinking, I jumped out of the boat, crying and calling to Him as I swam to the shore.

When the others arrived in the boat, Jesus had the fire going and said He would cook some of the fish for us. I went on the boat and grabbed the nets. There were 153 fish, and yet the net was not torn.

We cooked the fish and ate bread. Everything felt right again and we were home. None of us wanted breakfast to end.

But when I saw Jesus look at me again, I was afraid. We had not yet talked of my betrayal.

Jesus said, "Peter, do you love Me?"

I've never wanted to convince anyone of anything the way I did on that day. I wanted Him to know, but I had boasted in the past of my love for Him and I had failed to live up to my bold claims.

"Of course. You know I love You."

"Then feed My sheep.

"Do you love Me, Peter?

"Go feed My sheep.

"Do you love Me, Peter?

"Go feed My sheep."

It was as if He was saying, "You—the most sinful one—you go build My church. Because I know you now go with great humility, you go with a fresh understanding that there is a loving God and you are not Him. You go wearing the grace you will give away."

I didn't know how He could ever want me to display Him, but I was in.

The Stream of Calling

The Bible is not a book about lovely, perfect people. It's a book full of the most messed-up people of all generations, and yet God moves through them.

God has always been in the business of taking the foolish things to shame the wise and taking the broken, imperfect people to display His glory.[1]

It was after Peter's darkest moment that he had the greatest impact.

Jesus comes near to Peter in his brokenness. He shows His power once again through Peter's inadequacy. He cooks for the disciples. He eats with them. He hangs by the fire with them. And then He asks Peter to feed others, to pass on the love he's received. Jesus had a message for Peter, for us: all we have, all we do, comes through Him—and is meant to be shared in fellowship with Him. This is who Jesus is and this is what He wants for all of us. He wants us to be with Him and then give away what we have been given from being with Him. When you connect with God like that, He gets really contagious to everybody else.

When I first embraced the audacious call to disciple a generation, somehow I believed God wanted to use my gifts and effort. But that was never going to be my story. And I am not alone. That was never the story of anyone used mightily by God, even in biblical times. That will never be the story of anyone used mightily by God. From Moses, the stutterer who freed a nation, to David, the adulterer who was a man after God's heart, to Rahab, a prostitute who became the hero of Israel, to Harriet Tubman, a former uneducated slave who freed hundreds, to Mother Teresa, a tiny woman who took on the greatest needs in the world. It's the "least of these" that He best likes to use, so if you feel like you are not enough, celebrate! And be thankful that you get to be free of the weight of trying to prove you have it all together. You are in company with the unqualified—those God is waiting to blow wildly through.

After my journey into Jesus's life and seeing all the ways He clearly issues more than enough to cover my weakness, my fears, my broken-ness, my failures, my general mess of a life, I finally believed God enough to make my trembly confession—*I am not enough*—into a blinding spotlight with over a million people watching.

Since then, since I've stopped trying to be enough, I've led better than ever before. I've had more fun. I've been more free. I've enjoyed working *with* God so much more than I could have imagined.

BUILDING LIGHT

The world's message is simple: You are enough. All on your own, you are enough. But that mantra fails us either because we deep down know we aren't enough or because our self-esteem inflates and we charge through life independent of God and people. Either outcome leaves us lonely and disappointed. Self-esteem is not the answer.

So why are we working so hard to do life, to make a difference all on our own?

John opens his gospel about Jesus with the incredible truth that God came for us and to us, and then he offers this incredible imagery of what Jesus would bring: the light shining into the darkness and becoming the light of men.[2]

When I think about light, every single light humans have ever built requires energy or some force to light it. Lightbulbs drain and run out, even LED lights eventually. Flashlights, car lights, lamps . . . they all pull energy from some other source that can drain or become depleted.

Then I think of the light God creates. Fire running wild, the sun burning always, bajillions of stars all burning with great force—all the light that He creates, it needs nothing to exist. It needs no other energy source. It just is.

When I think of our backpacks, when I think of our striving, I realize we've been trying to build light. I've been trying to produce light.

- We try to give God to people we love, strategizing perfect speeches rather than getting on our knees.
- We try to control and protect our lives from suffering rather than trust that God has good for us in all that He brings.
- We read every parenting book and try our best to build kids who love God and are protected from pain. And when they rebel or suffer, we forget that nearly all our personal journeys to God involved rebelling or pain.
- We start to control and do everything ourselves rather than risk others' involvement and their mistakes.
- We go through tragedy alone because we don't want to bother people, believing the lie that we don't need others' help in our darkest times.

And guess what happens when people try to produce light? We get tired. Trying drains energy, like every human light that has ever been created.

So what if instead of trying to create light, we simply received light? That sounds so much more fun to me, so much easier. We make lousy lights because we were built to enjoy and reflect light, not to produce light.

The vision of God for our lives is that we would receive His light and then give light to the world. In Matthew 5:14 Jesus says, "You are the light of the world." Most of the time, the New Testament refers to Jesus being the Light, but when His Spirit lives in us, we are the light of the world. We receive who Jesus is and then give Him away.

The degree to which we believe and embrace our identity as a Spirit-filled child of God will be the degree to which His light shines through us. We are God's and He is ours. He is in us and through us and with us. That is our identity. And it changes everything.

If we embraced our true identity, we wouldn't just rest from striving to do impossible things; we would sit in awe of this fierce, crazy, awesome Light that is not contained and that is fully accessible to us.

It reminds me of lying in bed next to Zac the night we first met Cooper as an almost-four-year-old in Rwanda. We both lay looking at the ceiling, barely in touch with some of the enormous challenges ahead. How do we parent a child who has never known love? From where is this unconditional love going to come? How do we discipline him while we are trying to make him feel secure? And how do we form in Cooper an identity as our son when he has never had a category for a mom or dad? Honestly, we didn't do nearly enough reading about adoption beforehand.

Then, staring at the ceiling, as if he had landed on a solution for the monumental parenting we had in front of us, Zac said, "To the degree that I am able to receive the unconditional love of a God who has adopted me into His family will be the degree that I can reflect that love to Cooper."

It is so simple and so difficult. Everything flows out of our identity. The front line of the battle in our souls isn't the fight to become something we aren't or hope to be; it is a battle to believe the One we belong to and who we are. And when we are settled and secure in that truth, the Light that fills us cannot help but shine forth.

When we aren't secure in our identity, our actions toward others become more about pride and performance than service and ministry. Part of what always felt angsty to me about being in leadership was that if I was going to do it, then I wanted to knock it out of the park. Simple obedience to God wasn't enough; I wanted to be admired and incredible in the process.

When I read 1 Thessalonians 5:5—"You are all children of light, children of the day. We are not of the night or of the darkness"—I feel like God is saying, *Okay, Jennie, you can keep living like this, working so hard, striving to make your own light in the dark. Or you can walk into who you already are: My child, a child of the day, a child made to enjoy the sun. You can keep trying to be enough all the days of your life. Or you could quit. I promise you all those things you're craving: peace, joy, fun, not missing these moments with your kids who are growing so fast, enjoying Me again, deep connection with your people, My purposes for your day, confidence. I'm going to show you how to receive all of that. I will even show you how to give it away.*

I know it seems backward. You are just going to have to trust me. Jesus's opposite ways actually work.

BUILDING FRUIT

Friend, you and I are invited to be part of an epic, awesome eternal work, but many of us are missing out because we are still trying to measure up and trying to do it in our own strength. So how are we going to do this? How are we going to leave and change and be different?

We do it by taking seriously the words of Jesus in John 15: "Abide in me, and I in you. As the branch cannot bear fruit by itself, unless it abides in the vine, neither can you, unless you abide in me. I am the vine; you are the branches. Whoever abides in me and I in him, he it is that bears much fruit, for apart from me you can do nothing."[3]

Our directive from God is clear and simple: *Cease striving. Abide in Me. I produce the fruit. You don't have to work so hard at this. You can feel urgent for My people and yet keep still in your soul. You can abide. You don't have to run so hard.*

In fact, it's pretty funny that we think we can build fruit.

Have you ever had a pear from Harry & David, the food and gift company?

These pears alone—the existence of juicy pears this perfect—are evidence there is a God. True? I ordered them for somebody this week, and she almost cried she loved them so much. These pears really are just one of the greatest gifts.

Anyway, when you eat that pear, you know there has to be a God. A cold, perfectly ripe, juicy pear. No man named Harry or David could build these. Humans simply cannot create something like this.

God builds the sweetest, most incredible tasting thing on earth—and it is better than all the man-made processed food in the world. Real pears taste amazing and they're for our good and they show God's glory. In the same way, fruit like eternity-impacting relationships, conversations, and actions will emerge naturally as we seek Him, love Him, spend time with Him, abide in Him.

Let me just tell you what we're doing instead: we are building Nutter Butters. Humans don't create fruit; we build Nutter Butters. And they taste good. I like them a lot. But everyone is getting sick on the processed sugar we're handing out in the form of self-help strategies and self-esteem boosts. God gave us a great identity in which we can find deep security and confidence, but it only comes from who He is and what He has done for us.

Let me be abundantly clear: we really don't need to secure our identity; we need to be knocked over by our God. When we grow in our worship, we forget ourselves. Fixing our eyes on our God consumes us with Him and we couldn't care less if our identity is all sorted out.

We will live and love out of our view of God.

So we have to lay down some things. We have to lay down our striving and our performing and our pretending and our works that we think are proving our value to other people and to our God. It may be the most counterintuitive thing you will ever do.

But honestly, all those things tend to fall away when we stand before our unimaginable God.

So then really all we need to do is be with Him.

Being with Jesus, who is the vine, moves water and nourishment into and through us as branches. Connection to Him is how our thirsty souls are quenched and also how we receive a steady supply of the water required to produce mature, sweet-tasting fruit.

If a fruit tree doesn't receive sufficient water, the fruit it's producing will be sour or dry tasting or even just fall off rather than growing to maturity. An adequate amount of moisture is absolutely necessary to produce the sugars that create an incredible, fully ripened fruit.[4]

For our lives to yield fruit that is appealing and eternal, we need a constant supply of God, His rushing, wild, satisfying water contained in just who He is and poured out on us by our simply being near to Him, knowing Him, pressing up close to His Word and to His presence.

QUIETLY CHANGING THE WORLD

Recently I was watching a movie about the early church. Jesus has just ascended into heaven, and Peter and all the disciples are in the same upper room where Jesus washed their feet. They don't know what to do.

Someone looks at Peter and asks, "If Jesus were still here, what would He do?"

The future church stands in the balance.

I am sitting there watching this moment, wondering, *What is Peter, the person the church of God will be built upon, going to say? What do they do first? They are waiting for the Helper Jesus promised. What do they do first to build a movement to reach the world? It needs to be big and epic and creative and strategic.*

Then do you know what he said? "We pray."

In my bedroom, in my plaid pajama pants with my daughter next to me watching that movie, I just started weeping. When Peter said, "We pray," my fear and striving just melted away.

We do not change the world with might and power and creative strategies.

We watch God change the world when we pray and abide and believe.

That's what we do. We believe God is real and we talk to Him.

The lie is this: if it isn't big, it doesn't matter. Then because we believe it, we make influence the goal rather than loving God and people with all of our gifts and life.

If you make influence your goal, your heart will become consumed with what the world thinks. You'll miss the Holy Spirit's incredible work right in front of you, your soul will get so sick because it will never be satisfied, and rather than give God away through your gifts, you will use Him to get somewhere.

"Make it your ambition to lead a quiet life, to mind your own business and to work with your hands."[5] May we desire to be helpful rather than important. May we seek to make God's name great and not our own.

I don't want to set my eyes on impact; I want to set my eyes on Jesus and knowing Him more.

As the disciples prayed, the Holy Spirit was given, and then their mission and purpose was so simple and clear. They just walked outside and started preaching Jesus, and they knelt beside the sick and healed them. They told everyone, "The Messiah has come. He is real. He is risen. You don't want to miss this."

For the first time in all of history, the church and the Spirit of Christ were on the loose and the Spirit was with His people and in them. That is THE story, and if you think for a second it has changed from that day, it has not. Nothing is different.

What are we not believing about God?

Are we trying to do the work of God without God?

I picture our generation of God's people, and we are performing and building platforms or hiding in the back afraid. We aren't looking at God; we are looking at each other.

I picture God saying, *If My people would call on My name and they would confess their sins and believe Me, I would free them and move through them in ways they can't imagine.*

That's the story; that is God's plan. The way we get to join right now? We quit trying to be great and just let God be great through us.

See, I want to be the disciple who walks out of my time with God full of the Holy Spirit and heads down the stairs to the people who need Jesus and proclaims Him without end until I die. And not because I'm striving, but because the Holy Spirit is in me and has changed me, and what else would I do but go tell everyone I know about a God who saves us from ourselves and our sin?

One night when I was doubting my calling and gifts, rather than flatter me and build my shaky self-esteem, Zac sent me this quote from Charles Haddon Spurgeon:

> We would have it so happen that, when our life's history is written, whoever reads it will not think of us as "self-made men," but as the handiwork of God, in whom his grace is magnified. Not in us may men see the clay, but the Potter's

hand. They said of one, "He is a fine preacher"; but of another they said, "We never notice how he preaches, but we feel that God is great." We wish our whole life to be a sacrifice; an altar of incense continually smoking with sweet perfume unto the Most High.[6]

To simply display God has become my greatest goal. What could be a greater calling than to live so that God's great grace is magnified in our lives? Like Peter, we go feed His sheep with the truth of God's forgiveness and grace and love and power. Not with flashy gifts and speeches, but in our weakness, because our aim is to build the Name that won't ever die.

THE SMALL, SIMPLE THINGS

We abide, yes. It seems nearly passive. But notice that immediately after Jesus talks about abiding in John 15, He talks about fruitfulness. The danger of accepting God's enoughness is that we would become complacent. We would feel like He had it all covered so we wouldn't need to do anything.

While we have overcomplicated our calling, the solution is not swinging to nothingness and checking out and disabling the work of God through our lives. People need our God, and we are the method God chose to display Himself. We just realize we are empowered by the God of the universe to go and do the work. Again, the way we move forward in this is awfully simple and backward. You ready?

We quit being afraid to do the simple things Jesus said to do.

What did He say to do? He said,

We pray.

We hold tightly to His Word.[7]

We love Him with all of our heart, soul, mind, and strength
instead of pretending as if we do.[8]

We love our neighbor.[9]

He didn't say fight every cultural battle of your day, because He knew the fights of this world will pass away. No matter how important the cultural fight is, guess what? In heaven it will not matter.

We fight for people to believe God. In fact, it all boils down to this: Abide and love.

See, I love John 15 because He gives us such a picture of how this is going to work. He says, *Listen. You stick with Me, you abide with Me, you pray, you read the Word, you be with Me, love Me, stay near. You're just going to be this little branch. I'll build fruit. I'll build it through you.*

He has a big vision for us, but He will cause the big part to happen. He says, *You're going to display Me. I'm going to go up to heaven, I'm going to give Myself to you in the form of the Spirit, and you're going to go out and I will grow fruit through you.*

I read in the book of Acts about the disciples after the Holy Spirit has filled them, and I want what they have. And then I realize I have what they had.

After Jesus so freely forgave Peter and then gave him a mission there on the beach, the disciple finally had a fierce peace that caused him to stop fighting for his place and start fighting to free people. A single-mindedness flooded him with peace and joy and connectedness and presence and mission and confidence and rest. All of that is ours too, yours and mine, as we seek to make a difference in a hurting world.

So what do we do?

I want you to feel like you can walk away and it isn't just that your soul shifts, but you actually know what to do when you feel yourself trying to measure up. When you feel yourself feeling like you are not enough. When you feel yourself moving into that kind of sad place of *What do I do? I feel paralyzed and I don't know what to do.*

Do you know what happens when we go to meet with Jesus? When we are with Him in His presence? When we are in His Word and we are memorizing it? When we are in our local churches and we are in authentic community and we're honest about our struggles and not pretending or performing?

No darkness can stand against us.

Nothing can stand against the force of God moving through a soul completely in love with Him.

It is the simple things that will change the world.

It is the old, unclever things that will change your soul.

You sit down every day with Him in His Word, you look eye to eye with a small group of people, and you tell the truth about your soul. You don't leave the church. You build the church. You do the simple work of loving God and loving people. It is messy, hard, not too glamorous. And that sounds like Jesus.

To Know Him and Love Him and Give Him Away

There is a hungry, thirsty world out there, and they long for their lives to mean something. Your neighbors are going through divorces, the death of children, abuse, and they pray at night that there is a God. You can take Him to them. Do not miss getting to give God away to people. It is what we were built for. We use our gifts, somehow, some way, anywhere, any time. Forget about size or numbers or reach.

Oh, I fear we have glamorized what it means to follow Jesus. We think it happens on stages and in books and on blogs, but it happens around tables, throughout neighborhoods, and in living rooms. I bet the top five people who have changed your life were eye to eye across from you, investing time in your life.

You want to know what the big thing is? It is one person sitting with one person and opening the Bible and saying, "Do you know Jesus?" That is the big stuff.

Then I think about all the excuses we give ourselves about why He could never go out through us. It's the story of my whole life. These are still the lies that I fight: We are not enough. We don't have enough. There is not enough.

But then I think about being part of this epic story of God. Can you imagine?

He is waiting. He is waiting and He wants to go crazy through you. You don't feel like you measure up? Then you are exactly who God is looking for. You are the one. You are the one He is after. He wants you and me: the losers, the broken, the sinful, the ones who know and accept how great is our need of Him. That is how He works. Every single person in the Bible, besides Jesus, was broken, afraid, insecure, fearful, busy, did not have enough time, did not have enough money, did not have enough of anything—and God moved through them to change history.

Eternity is going to be shifted. Because finally a little army decided nothing on earth would hold them back.

Just how will eternity change?

Many new people, new ideas, new buzzwords, new strategies will rise up and claim to be the answer to our thirst and to changing the world for God. But it is in the old, quiet connection to the vine that power flows. Jesus is with you. He is for you. And the only way we will enjoy the work and joy He has for us here is to do life with Him!

Make it your goal to love and know Jesus as much as humanly possible and ministry *will* happen.

Jesus lays this out to His disciples so beautifully for us in John 15–16. I want to launch you into the world with a crystal-clear vision of how we live out the awesome calling of God for our lives, and so I took Jesus's words and rewrote the heart of it here.

Hear His heart and vision for you:

There is so much I have taught you, so much I have shown you, but I want to make plain the most urgent thing. I want you to understand what it means to do this life without Me here beside you. Trust Me, it is better if I go away. I will send a Helper who will fill you, equip you, remind you, stick with you. This relationship with Me is just beginning.

Let Me tell you how to enjoy it as your lives unfold. Because here, in this world you will have trouble. But take heart; I have overcome the world.

Do you remember when we walked through the vineyards together? We saw the vinedresser pruning back the branches. That is how the Father tends to you, cutting you back. It is painful and may seem unjust at times, but He only cuts back the branches He loves. Do not fear pain; receive it and watch as it causes much more fruit to be born through you.

Do not strive to produce fruit. It is impossible. I am the Vine and the Source; you are simply the branches, attached to Me. As you stay near to Me, intimately close to Me, I will flood you with nourishment, with life, with peace and joy, and your little branch lives will bear an abundance of fruit. This is how it works.

If we don't stay connected, you will wither up. You will feel empty and thirsty and overwhelmed with this life and your sin, and you certainly can't help anyone else. But if you remain in Me and near Me, I will not only give you water and life; I will build healthy life-giving fruit through you. The overflowing wine, the spring of water welling up, the miraculous bread for the hungry, the healing and rest you long for, the power and hope over death—all of this will pour into you and through you to a starving, thirsty world.

But never forget where all of this and more is found.

Remember, it is only in Me, with Me, through Me, because of Me that you have life to enjoy and give away.

"Make yourselves at home in my love. If you keep my commands, you'll remain intimately at home in my love."[10]

—Jesus

EXPERIENCE GUIDE

BE STILL

Therefore, if anyone is in Christ, he is a new creation. The old has passed away; behold, the new has come. All this is from God, who through Christ reconciled us to himself and gave us the ministry of reconciliation.

2 Corinthians 5:17–18

Goodness, I believe in you! I just know that Jesus can shift the world through you. As we wrap up here, dream big and imagine how God could move as you set down this book. What are your hopes and dreams?

STEP INTO
THE STREAM

When you put down this book,
what will be your first step of
obedience?

WADE IN DEEPER

Write a letter to yourself. Tell yourself

- what you hope for,

- what you are leaving behind,

- what has changed in your view of Christ
  through reading this book, and

- where you hope to be in one year.

QUENCH YOUR THIRST

The lie you are rejecting is _____.
The truth you are believing is that Jesus is
enough for _____.

THE OVERFLOW

How could you give this truth away
to someone this week?

....

What We Believe About God

We began this journey clear that there is an enemy trying to take us out. But we end in a different place. We don't end focused on an enemy or even focused on ourselves. We end focused on our God. Who He is frees us; who He is flows in and through us and changes everything.

And who one day will ultimately and finally quench our deepest thirst. Revelation describes that day, "Then the angel showed me the river of the water of life, bright as crystal, flowing from the throne of God and of the Lamb through the middle of the street of the city."[1] It is coming.

In the meantime, let your thirst remind you to come back to the only One who can quench it.

I'm convinced that we could be a generation who lives by faith, full of it, overwhelmed with God and focused on Him rather than our sufficiency and trying to prove ourselves in this short breath of a life. We have a mission and a glorious God who is wholly available to us.

As we step into His streams of abundance, we live in freedom and peace. No more bondage. No more striving. No more performing.

Everything we crave flows into us from our Creator God who adores us. We walk forward with bold, audacious belief in what He declares about Himself and about us:[2]

I AM WHO I AM.

I am the beginning and the end.
I am the first, and I am the last.

I am light; in Me there is no darkness at all.

My hand laid the foundation of the earth,
and my right hand spread out the heavens;
when I call to them,
they stand forth together.

Before I formed you in the womb I knew you.

I chose you and appointed you that you should go
and bear fruit and that your fruit should abide,
so that whatever you ask the Father in my name,
he may give it to you.

I am He who blots out your mistakes . . .
I will not remember your sins.

All who receive Me,
who believe in My name,
I give the right to become children of God.

Do you not know that you are God's temple
and that God's Spirit dwells in you?

My Spirit is with you.

I will not leave you.

I will equip you for every good work I've planned.

I did not give you a spirit of fear
but of power, love, and self-control.

I will build My church through you,
and the gates of hell will not overcome it.

I will comfort you as you wait.

I will remind you this is all real.

I am on My way.

My steadfast love endures forever and ever.

In just a little while . . .
I am coming, and I will take you to the place I am.

You will inherit the earth.

You will be with Me.
I will wipe every tear from your eyes and death will be no more.
Behold, I am making all things new.

My kingdom is coming.
My will shall be done on earth as it is in heaven.

Acknowledgments

There was a time in my life that I would pray for God's help, expecting it to come straight from Him in some mysterious way, but now I know that His provisions very often come through His people. Right before this book was due, one of those people, Jonathan Merritt, boldly challenged me that I was writing the wrong book. No doubt, I was, but with three weeks to turn it in, scrapping a year of work and starting over felt like insanity.

Yet as I walked around the dirt trail near our office with my dear friend Lindsey Nobles, who always helps me embrace the crazy things God calls me to do, I knew he was right. And so the adventure of writing a new book with all of my soul began. These words would cost me and the people around me more than any have. You see, writing is a ginormous group project where one person usually gets the credit.

So here is my attempt to rectify that.

First, God: You never let me get comfortable. And while I get so mad about that sometimes, I actually adore it about You, because I know uncomfortable is where I need You. So thank You for pushing me once again and yet being in it with me every second. You are a trustworthy good Ox. And I so enjoy living and working with You. I pray these words did You even the tiniest bit of justice.

Zac: You are my best friend; you are my safe place. You let me be crazy, even when it costs you. You fill in the gaps and yet never act like

I am leaving any gaps. You are the most amazing husband and friend I could imagine. I'm thankful we paid our dues early in marriage so we can enjoy these years of it. Friend, you know this book wouldn't happen without you. And it sure wouldn't be as good. You make me better, and you made this work better!

Conner, Kate, Caroline, and Coop: Your faith in God and support of me showed up the past few months. This book cost you the most. And yet, as always, you rallied. You believe in me and you cheer for me. You are the least selfish bunch of kids on earth. I am so proud to be your mom.

My family: Mom and Dad, you are just the greatest two parents on the face of the earth. You could not be more supportive, and I am so grateful God gave me you! And Carolyn and Randy, you are two of the most incredible cheerleaders in our lives. And all of you are the best grandparents to our kids. They are so blessed to have all four of you! Thank you. And Ashley, you are my other sister. Sitting on the beach with you shaped these words too. Phone calls with you spark my love for God. You are such a treasure to me.

My friends: Thanks for not quitting on me. There are too many of you to mention all by name but specifically Lindsey Nobles, Bekah Self, Sarah Henry, Julie Manning, Jessica Honegger, and Laura Choy. You all are daily support to me, and I cannot imagine my life without you. Thanks for helping me be brave and kicking me in the pants when I screw up. Forever grateful for you.

My IF:Gathering family: I never dreamed of the family that IF would bring into my life. From sisters around the world to people who fill the office I love to walk into every day. In every way this is for you and because of you. And a special thanks to my team in Austin: Lindsey Nobles, Jordyn Perry, Hannah Warren, Jordan Todd, Sam Littlefield, Jordan Paden, Bre Lee, Amy Brown, Brooke Mazzariello, Lisa Huntsberry, Aly Bonville, Kelsey Harp, Lauren Sterrett, Elizabeth Milburn, Rachel Lindholm, and Melissa Zalvidar for brainstorming and running up to Gruene to help me get unstuck, for patience while I miss meetings *again* for edits, for being in it with me, for transcribing talks, for running my computer cord up when I was on a roll, and for holding down the fort so beautifully. Elizabeth and Melissa, you two did a lot of grunt work for this book. *Thank you all!*

The Yates and Yates team: Here I am again thanking you. Nothing about you is halfhearted. You are just all in! It is such a picture of the body of Christ. You spend so much time using your individual gifts behind the scenes to be sure that this is the right message and the best way to display God. Curtis and Karen, you are family to us. And I cannot imagine if we hadn't met so many years ago; our lives would not be the same.

WaterBrook: Goodness, from our first meeting, I thought you were too good to be true. You all had bigger dreams than I did (and that is saying something), and you so passionately believed in me. You have given me your all, you have shown up, you have thought out of the box about reaching women, you have supported me, even when I get all crazy on you and change the book last minute. I honestly could not ask for a better team.

My editor, Laura Barker: When someone decides to wildly write a book in three weeks, the passion is there, the message is there, but it is a train wreck! Laura, you deserve more than anyone to have your name on the cover for the hours and days and weeks you spent poring over every word, helping me think better, and pushing me beyond what I thought I could do. I cannot thank you enough for being in this with me. I can say with integrity this book would not exist without you.

My church family at Austin Stone: Thanks for quietly being this force in my life. You feed me Jesus each week. No doubt your influence in my life is all over these pages, Halim, Matt, Kevin, and others. I love that I find myself in a church that values the Word of God and the gospel above all else. You consistently bring me back to Jesus. And Val Vance, thank you for your part in these words as well.

Chad's team: Thank you, Katy, Haley, and Chad Cannon.

And finally, Our Village: How could a Facebook group become a family? But it did. You lost sleep, thought deeply, and prayed and cheered when I most needed you. You were God's love to me again and again! Grateful.

Notes

·····························

Admitting Our Thirst

1. Ben Rector, "If You Can Hear Me," *The Walking In Between,* Aptly Named Records/ROAR, 2013.
2. Jeremiah 2:13, NIV.
3. John 7:37–38, NIV.

Chapter 1: My Quiet Confession

1. Romans 3:23.

Chapter 2: Star Charts and Backpacks

1. Jeremiah 9:23–24.
2. 2 Corinthians 10:5, NIV.
3. See Psalm 23:2–3.
4. Psalm 103:12, NLT.

Chapter 3: Numbing Out

1. See Matthew 25:37–40.
2. See Matthew 11:28–30.

Chapter 4: Coming Up for Air

1. 1 John 2:6, NIV.
2. John 1:1–5, 9–14.
3. John 7:37–38, NIV.
4. Isaiah 41:10.
5. 2 Corinthians 12:9.

Chapter 5: No Longer Thirsty

1. See Luke 22:19–20; 1 Corinthians 11:23–25.
2. Hebrews 8:10–13.
3. See www.dictionary.com, s. vv. "joy," "entertainment."
4. See Psalm 84:10.
5. See Matthew 5:29–30, 18:8; Mark 9:43–47.
6. See Psalm 63:1.
7. C. S. Lewis, *Mere Christianity* (New York: HarperCollins, 1980), 136–37.

Chapter 6: No Longer Lonely

1. Mandy Len Catron, "To Fall in Love with Anyone, Do This," *New York Times,* January 9, 2015, www .nytimes.com/2015/01/11 /fashion/modern-love-to-fall -in-love-with-anyone-do-this .html.

2. Jean Vanier, *Becoming Human* (Toronto: Anansi, 2008), 7–8.

3. C. S. Lewis, *The Four Loves* (Orlando: Harcourt Brace, 1988), 121.

Chapter 7: No Longer Tired

1. See Matthew 8:23–27.

2. See John 6:5–6.

3. See Exodus 3–4.

4. See John 6:29.

5. Isaiah 30:15.

Chapter 8: No Longer Passive

1. John 9:39.

Chapter 9: No Longer Afraid

1. See Romans 5:3–5, NIV.

2. See Philippians 3:8–9, NIV.

3. John 11:15.

4. Psalm 19:1.

5. Ephesians 2:4–5.

6. Philippians 4:12, NIV.

7. See Philippians 4:13.

8. Oswald Chambers, "The Big Compelling of God," *Called of God* (Grand Rapids: Discovery House, 2015), e-book.

9. See John 14:3.

10. Romans 8:35, 37–39.

Chapter 10: No Longer Ashamed

1. 2 Corinthians 10:5.

2. James 5:16, NIV.

3. 1 John 1:8–9.

Chapter 11: No Longer Empty

1. See 1 Corinthians 1:27.

2. See John 1:4–5.

3. John 15:4–5.

4. Rick LaVasseur, "How Does a Fruit Tree Produce Fruit?," Quora, October 23, 2012, www.quora.com

/How-does-a-fruit
-tree-produce-fruit.

5. 1 Thessalonians 4:11, NIV.
6. Charles Spurgeon, quoted in
   Godfrey Holden Pike and
   James Champlin Fernald,
   "The Last Sermon," *Charles
   Haddon Spurgeon, Preacher,
   Author, Philanthropist: With
   Anecdotal Reminiscences*
   (New York: Funk & Wag-
   nalls, 1892), 397.
7. See Hebrews 10:23.
8. See Mark 12:30.
9. See Mark 12:31.
10. John 15:9–10, MSG.

*Final Thoughts: What We
Believe About God*

1. Revelation 22:1–2.
2. See Exodus 3:14; Revelation
   22:13; 1 John 1:5; Isaiah
   48:13; Jeremiah 1:5; John
   15:16; Isaiah 43:25; John
   1:12; 1 Corinthians 3:16;
   Ezekiel 36:26–27; Deuter-
   onomy 31:8; Hebrews 13:21;
   2 Timothy 1:7; Matthew
   16:18; Isaiah 66:13; John
   14:26; Revelation 3:11;
   Psalm 138:8; Hebrews
   10:37; Psalm 25:13; Revelation 21:3–5; Matthew 6:10.

Book Club Resources

Can I just say how in awe I am of God and how He works? I am praying that you feel God's love for you in these words. I am convinced He wants to draw you closer so He can move in and through you in ways you could never begin to imagine!

It's exciting to envision groups gathering to talk about His streams of grace and the life Jesus invites us to—which is exactly what I hoped for when I sat down to write this book. I dared to picture you and your friends sharing honestly about the places you're tempted to strive, the ways you tend to numb out, and all the ways you don't measure up—and discovering together what it means to let Jesus be your enough.

If reading this book brought hope and healing to the hurting places in your life, if you found satisfaction for your soul-deep thirst, please invite a group of friends to share the experience and step into the freedom that comes from drawing near to Jesus and His Word.

Even if you're not part of a regular book club, I hope you'll grab some friends and spend an evening (or several) talking, eating, laughing, praying, and learning together. It doesn't have to be fancy or formal. Remember: we've got nothing to prove! To make things even easier, I've included in the following pages some discussion questions as well as a few of my family's favorite girls' night recipes.

I'd love to hear about your group's conversations through Facebook or Instagram. I know your words will help remind me each day that the goal is to know and love Jesus as much as humanly possible.

Together let's love God and let Him love this hungry, thirsty world through us. I can't wait to see what He does!

Jennie

Discussion Questions

I love a discussion that goes deep fast and helps us connect and challenge one another. That's why I encourage you to have a free-flowing conversation with your group over which truths in this book have grabbed hold of you and shifted your perspective about what it means to live with God instead of striving to impress Him. But for those who love a bit of structure, at least to get things rolling, here are some questions to guide your discussion through some of the core ideas of *Nothing to Prove*. Spread these questions out over a few weeks if you are meeting several times.

1. In what area(s) of your life are you experiencing a soul-deep thirst? Where do you usually turn in your attempts to satisfy that craving?

2. What aspect of your world currently requires more than you can deliver? How would it feel to let go of your striving in that area and simply admit you aren't enough? Terrifying or freeing?

3. "God is not after great performances or great movements. He is after us!" In what ways does this truth align with or challenge your view of God's expectations for you?

4. What symptoms of numbing out do you recognize in yourself? When you consider your life—both the mundane parts and the bigger moments—as part of God's grand eternal story unfolding, how does that shift your perspective?

5. "The point is to know God more and to give Him away." What emotions and ideas are triggered when you consider the implications of this sentence for your daily priorities?

6. What receives most of your time, thought, and energy? How do you think that affects your search for true satisfaction? What would it look like in practical terms to find your joy in Jesus?

7. "In our pursuit of deep connection, we have to recognize that we can often look to good things like community, authenticity, confession to take the place of connecting with Jesus." What or who is most likely to take the place of Jesus in your life? What would it take for you to stop hiding and see yourself in God's eyes, fully known and accepted? How might that transform your relationships with other people?

8. It feels so counterintuitive, particularly in today's culture of busyness and stress, to stop striving and simply rest. Think about a situation that keeps you awake at night. What would happen if you made the choice to let go and trust God to accomplish His purposes?

9. Describe a time you witnessed someone else take a risk in obedience to God. What was the result? What fears prevent you from engaging in activities and relationships that reveal God's glory? What risk are you willing to take this week to be part of God's story line of healing and beauty?

10. There are no easy answers to the inevitable struggles we will face, but if we truly believe Christ pours His love into our suffering, we need to live based on that promise. Where do you see streams of hope breaking through the bleak areas in your life? How can you help others see the first hints of light in the middle of the darkness in their own lives?

11. "We are not defined by our worst or our best; we are defined by our God." What pieces of your past have you kept hidden away in the darkest corners of your heart? What fears keep you from bringing them to Christ? How can your friends support you in laying your dirt before God?

12. We live in a hungry, thirsty world, but we can't give people God unless we first grab hold of Him ourselves. What would change in your life if your daily goal was to know and love Jesus as much as humanly possible? How would it shape your priorities, your relationships, your ministry, your sense of purpose, your experience of peace?

13. Which of God's declarations at the end of the book (see pages 233–35) resonates most clearly for you today, and why?